Lecture Notes in Artificial In

Subseries of Lecture Notes in Computer {

Edited by J. G. Carbonell and J. Siekmann

Lecture Notes in Computer Science

Edited by G. Goos, J. Hartmanis and J. van Leeuwen

Springer

Berlin
Heidelberg
New York
Barcelona
Budapest
Hong Kong
London
Milan
Paris
Santa Clara
Singapore
Tokyo

Alexander Franz

Automatic Ambiguity Resolution in Natural Language Processing

An Empirical Approach

Springer

Series Editors
Jaime G. Carbonell, Carnegie Mellon University, Pittsburgh, PA, USA
Jörg Siekmann, University of Saarland, Saarbrücken, Germany

Author

Alexander Franz
Sony Corporation, D-21 Laboratory
6-7-35 Kitashinagawa, Shinigawa-Ku, Tokyo 141, Japan
E-mail: amf@pdp.crl.sony.co.jp

Cataloging-in-Publication Data applied for

Die Deutsche Bibliothek - CIP-Einheitsaufnahme

Franz, Alexander:
Automatic ambiguity resolution in natural language processing :
an empirical approach / Alexander Franz. - Berlin ; Heidelberg
; New York ; Barcelona ; Budapest ; Hong Kong ; London ;
Milan ; Paris ; Santa Clara ; Singapore ; Tokyo : Springer, 1996
  (Lecture notes in computer science ; Vol. 1171 : Lecture notes in
  artificial intelligence)
  ISBN 3-540-62004-4
NE: GT

CR Subject Classification (1991): I.2.7, I.2, I.6.5, G.3, F.4.2-3

ISBN 3-540-62004-4 Springer-Verlag Berlin Heidelberg New York

© Springer-Verlag Berlin Heidelberg 1996
Printed in Germany

Typesetting: Camera ready by author
SPIN 10549137   06/3142 – 5 4 3 2 1 0   Printed on acid-free paper

Foreword

Natural language processing is often called an "AI-complete" task, in the sense that in order to truly process language (i.e. to comprehend, to translate, to generate) full understanding is required, which is itself the ultimate goal of Artificial Intelligence. For those who seek solutions to practical problems, this is not a desirable property of NLP. However, it is possible to address reduced versions of the NLP problem without the prerequisite of having first solved all of the other arbitrarily-difficult AI problems. There are various ways to restrict the NLP problem: restrict the semantic domain, restrict the expressiveness of the syntax, focus on only one aspect of NLP at a time (e.g. phoneme recognition, Part-of-Speech tagging, morphological analysis), seek only approximate solutions (e.g. by replacing a complex cognitive model with a statistical component), and so on. The work described in this monograph pursues the latter two approaches with significant success.

The beauty of statistical techniques for NLP is that in principle they require only training data — not manual reprogramming — to solve new or extended versions of the same problem. For instance, a Part-of-Speech tagger should be as easily trainable for any subset of English (e.g. legal, medical, engineering texts) as for the original subset in which it was developed. Moreover, it should be applicable to other languages as well, after modifying the tagset and possibly the feature set. The drawbacks of statistical systems, however, are also significant. It is difficult to solve the more complex NLP problems statistically with acceptable accuracy. It is difficult to obtain enough training data for models with large feature sets. It is a significant challenge to create computationally-tractable models that cope with significant combinations of features. And, it is seldom clear a priori how to design the feature set or what statistical model to use. All these difficulties notwithstanding, significant progress has been made in statistical methods for speech recognition, Part-of-Speech tagging, lexical disambiguation, Prepositional Phrase (PP) attachment, and even end-to-end machine translation.

Dr. Franz's contribution is to develop a statistical paradigm for NLP tasks that makes minimal restrictive a priori assumptions. Based on loglinear modeling with contingency tables, the key idea is to be able to explore models that consider features singly, in pairs, or in larger interacting subsets, rather than in a single pre-determined and often suboptimal manner. Of course, this approach requires careful selection of potentially meaningful features, as well as certain simplifying assumptions – such as feature partitioning – to achieve computational tractability. The results on Part-of-Speech tagging and multiple-PP attachment structural disambiguation show the advances of this modeling approach over the previous state of the art. Of course much more remains to be investigated with respect to statistical NLP and hybrid rule-based/statistical approaches, but the methodology of the research and clear initial advances have been established.

September 1996   Jaime Carbonell

Preface

This is an exciting time for Artificial Intelligence (AI), and for Natural Language Processing (NLP) in particular. Within the last five years or so, a newly revived spirit has gained prominence that promises to revitalize our field: the spirit of empiricism.

As described by Cohen (1995), the revival of empiricism can be felt throughout all of AI. For NLP, empiricism offers a new orientation and a new way of looking at problems involving natural language that focuses on naturally-occurring language data.

There are three main aspects of the empirical approach to NLP. The first aspect concerns the *exploration* of the natural language phenomenon under study. Initial, pre-theoretical observations are analyzed and structured with respect to "features" or statistical variables. The data is examined for trends, and initial ideas about causal influences and interactions are formed.

The growing availability of online text and speech corpora has made it possible to perform such exploratory data analysis on natural language data. This enterprise has just begun, and much remains to be learned. Nevertheless, I expect that this type of activity will in time come to be widely accepted as an essential component of NLP methodology.

The second aspect of the empirical method is related to *model construction*. Currently, many models in empirical NLP are statistical models of the simplest type, implicitly assuming one of the common statistical distributions and estimating parameters directly from the observed training data.

This is mostly a reflection of the youth of the empirical NLP enterprise. After collecting, exploring, and structuring data, fitting a standard statistical model is the most obvious next step. In the future, I expect that the models will become more complex, combining both symbolic and statistical elements. This is likely to develop into a major research focus.

The third aspect of the empirical approach is probably the most familiar. It relates to *formal experiments*, statistical hypothesis testing, and the rejection or confirmation of scientific hypotheses. In the so-called hard sciences, this has long been a part of the standard methodology.

Not so in AI. Within NLP, even though formal hypothesis testing remains quite rare, this aspect of empiricism has already lead to a widespread concern with quantitative evaluation. At the current state of the art, the main concern usually lies with measuring the accuracy of a model at performing a specified task, such as recognizing a spoken word or determining the syntactic structure of a sentence.

If standardized data collections are used, then the accuracies obtained by different models can be compared directly, and conclusions about the fidelity of the different models can be drawn. This is currently not always the case, however; it is often difficult to interpret the reported accuracy measurements. As the field develops, I expect that there will be somewhat less of an emphasis on competition between different implemented systems, and a growing emphasis on drawing general conclusions about language processing.

In this book, we demonstrate the empirical approach to NLP by tackling one of the main problems in natural language analysis, the problem of automatic ambiguity resolution. Using data from the University of Pennsylvania Treebank, we investigate three particularly problematic types of syntactic ambiguity in English: unknown words, lexical Part-of-Speech ambiguity, and Prepositional Phrase attachment ambiguity.

It has often been suggested that effective ambiguity resolution requires the integration of multiple sources of knowledge. In this work, we will show how to construct procedures for automatic ambiguity resolution that achieve this aim in a precisely defined sense: By adopting the loglinear class of statistical models, we are able to take into account the interactions between different features, and thus obtain a Bayesian posterior probability distribution over the response variable that is properly conditioned on the combinations of the explanatory variables.

Our scientific result pertaining to the theory of natural language ambiguity can be summarized in one sentence: Ambiguity resolution procedures that take into account the interactions between analysis features obtain higher disambiguation accuracy than procedures that assume independence. This result is derived through a series of experiments that provide a rigorous evaluation of our models, and a thorough comparison with methods that have been described previously in the literature.

While this result does not *prove* that handling feature interactions is necessary, it certainly provides a strong indication. In doing so, this work suggests a number of avenues for further research on the theory of ambiguity resolution. At the same time, the techniques described here yield higher disambiguation accuracy than previously described methods, so they are directly useful for applied work on natural language analysis. More broadly, the methods for data analysis, modeling, and experimental evaluation that are described in this book are relevant to anyone working in NLP or AI.

This book is based on my PhD dissertation submitted to the Computational Linguistics Program at Carnegie Mellon University in 1995. I am deeply indebted to my advisor, Jaime Carbonell, for his continuous help, advice, and support. I am also grateful to the other members of my thesis committee, Ted Gibson, Michael "Fuzzy" Mauldin, and Teddy Seidenfeld, for their guidance and encouragement. I would like to thank my fellow Computational Linguistics graduate students; the members of the Computational Linguistics community in Pittsburgh; my friends and colleagues at the Center for Machine Translation and at Carnegie Group Inc.; Gerald Gazdar, who fostered my first interests in natural language; and the Sony research members. Finally, I wish to thank Keiko Horiguchi for making life wonderful.

Tokyo, September 1996   Alexander Franz

Table of Contents

List of Figures

List of Tables

1. Introduction

A natural language parsing system determines the structure of input text in a natural language, such as English or German. Ambiguity resolution is one of the main problems in natural language parsing. Ambiguity arises whenever an expression can be interpreted in more than one way. For example, consider the following actual newspaper headline:

British left waffles on Falklands $\qquad$ (1.1)

This expression can be interpreted in two different ways:

1. British commentators on the left of the political spectrum are engaging in "evasive, vague, or misleading speech or writing" on the issue of the Falkland islands.
2. British visitants to the Falkland islands left behind "light, crisp batter cakes".

Of course, the second interpretation sounds implausible, given knowledge of the Falklands conflict — but current natural language parsing systems do not have access to the vast amount of world knowledge required to make such a judgment. As another example, consider the following sentence:

Time flies like an arrow. $\qquad$ (1.2)

This sentence can be interpreted in at least the following ways:

1. Time passes along in the same manner as an arrow gliding through space.
2. I order you to take timing measurements on flies, in the same manner as you would time an arrow.
3. Fruit flies like to feast on a banana; in contrast, the species of flies known as "time flies" like an arrow.

In order to analyze expression such as these examples, it must be broken down into its parts or *constituents*, and the role that each constituent plays must be determined. During this process, the following questions need to be answered:

- What are the syntactic categories of the words? Are they nouns, verbs, adjectives, adverbs, etc.?

- What are the larger constituents of the sentence? For example, what noun phrases, verb phrases, prepositional phrases, and subordinate clauses occur in the sentence?
- How should the constituents be combined or *attached* to form the overall syntactic structure of the sentence?

Posed in isolation, these questions yield more than one answer, resulting in more than one possible interpretation. The word *waffles*, for example, can be a verb, or a noun. This is an instance of ambiguity.

This book describes an empirical approach to the automatic resolution of natural language ambiguity that is based on statistics gathered from online text corpora. Care has been taken to eliminate linguistic jargon from this survey, but some linguistic concepts may remain difficult to understand. For an accessible exposition of traditional English grammar, see [Quirk and Greenbaum, 1973]. The standard, exhaustive reference grammar is [Quirk et al., 1985]. Modern introductory textbooks of linguistics include [O'Grady et al., 1989] and [Finegan and Besnier, 1989]. For an overview of current research in Linguistics, see the four-book Cambridge Survey [Newmeyer, 1988]. For two expositions of current syntactic theories, see [Horrocks, 1987] and [Sells, 1985]. For clarification of linguistic terminology, refer to [Crystal, 1985].

1.1 Natural Language Ambiguity

Natural language parsing is the process of recovering the structure of natural language input. The remainder of this section explains what is involved in "recovering the structure" of a sentence, and why natural language ambiguity represents a stumbling block in this endeavour. For tutorial literature on natural language processing, see [Gazdar and Mellish, 1989], [Allen, 1995], and [Winograd, 1983].

Table 1.1. Levels of Linguistic Structure

Analysis Level	Explanation
Morphology	Structure of words
Phrase	Structure of noun phrases, adjective phrases, verb phrases, etc.
Clause	Structure of verb-argument combinations
Sentence	Structure of clause combinations
Modifier Attachment	Attachment of optional modifiers to phrases and to clauses

Sentences are not the only linguistic objects that possess internal structure. Other objects like words, clauses, and phrases are also structured. There resulting hierarchy of levels of linguistic structure is summarized in Figure 1.1; see [Winograd, 1983], chapter 1 for an elaboration. During parsing, the linguistic structure is recovered at each level of analysis.

Linguistics has documented significant regularities at each level of analysis. For example, take the following morphological regularity: In English, adding the suffix *-er* to a verb yields a noun that means "person who performs the act denoted by the noun". Thus, *play* yields *player*. An example of a syntactic regularity can be summarized as follows: In an English clause, the subject is usually found before the verb.

These regularities or *rules* are used during parsing to recover the structure of the input, and thereby to unravel the information encoded in the input. And this is where ambiguity comes in: Taking each level in isolation, more than one rule can be applied in many cases. For example, if there is a word ending in the suffix *-er*, it could be a noun of the type described above, but it could also be a comparative adjective. For example, the word *thinner* could be a comparative adjective (*this man is thinner than that man*), or a noun (*the paint thinner*).

Ambiguity occurs at each level of analysis, and it has the potential to multiply across levels. (Sometimes, other constraints only allow some possible interpretations.) This quickly results in a large number of possible interpretations for a single sentence. For example, [Martin et al., 1981] reports 455 different syntactic parses for the following sentence:

List the sales of the products produced in 1973 with the products   (1.3) produced in 1972.

There are many more decision points during natural language analysis that give rise to ambiguity, such as determining word-sense, subcategorization, complementation patterns, scope of quantification   and negation, and more. In this book, the discussion will be limited to Part-of-Speech ambiguity, the analysis of unknown words, and Prepositional Phrase attachment ambiguity. Each of these problems is treated as a case study, with detailed descriptions of a series of experiments that result in a series of statistical models with higher ambiguity resolution power than traditional methods.

1.2 Ambiguity and Robust Parsing

The research reported in this book work was motivated by the goal of robust, wide-coverage natural language analysis. The ability to parse open-ended text would benefit a number of areas in natural language processing, including information retrieval, data extraction from text, machine translation of unrestricted text, text summarization, text categorization, and more.

Many different techniques for natural language analysis have been described in the literature, ranging from AI methods like conceptual analysis

[Schank, 1975] to grammar-based techniques based on attribute-value formalisms such as HPSG [Pollard and Sag, 1987, Pollard and Sag, 1994]. But when these techniques are scaled up and applied to a wider range of vocabulary and grammatical structures, the parsing mechanisms are placed under severe strain by the weight of multiplying ambiguities.

There are a number of basic issues in natural language parsing. They involve determining how many different types of grammatical constructions should be covered, how much ambiguity arises as a result of more or less grammatical coverage, and determining the amount and nature of the information required to resolve the resulting ambiguities.

A primary tension holds between two needs: Maximizing coverage and minimizing resultant ambiguity. On the one hand, handling more text requires a wide-coverage grammatical model. On the other hand, wider coverage and more flexibility results in higher ambiguity.

1.2.1 Grammatical Coverage

In constructing a parsing grammar, a larger or smaller number of grammatical constructions can be covered. For example, the grammar can be tightly restricted to define the notion of "sentence" in terms of a small number of well-formed sentence structures, or it can be less restricted and also admit some fragmentary and incomplete structures. The more structures are allowed, the higher the coverage, but also the higher the potential ambiguity.

This point is best understood if we think of a grammar as a language model. A language model is a mathematical structure that represents some aspects of natural language. Certain parts of the model correspond to observable aspects of language. Via this correspondence, the model makes *predictions* about those aspects of language [Pollard, 1988]. For example, in speech recognition, a statistical language model is used to predict the probability of the next word, given a sequence of words. In linguistic theory, models based on methods from formal language theory are used to predict the grammaticality of a sentence. In HPSG, a calculus over typed feature structures is used to model the information content of linguistic signs.

The ambiguity inherent in a language model can be measured by the *perplexity* of the model.   Perplexity is a commonly used re-expression of entropy. (For an explanation of entropy, see Appendix A.) For more details on perplexity, see, for example, [Jelinek et al., 1977], and [Ferreti et al., 1990], who provide a discussion of some empirical shortcomings of perplexity in the context of speech recognition.

For our purpose, we can regard perplexity as an information-theoretic notion that is related to the number of choices available at each decision point of an information source, such as a language model. For an information source with entropy H, Perplexity is defined as 2^H. Intuitively, while entropy corresponds to the number of perfectly informative yes-no questions that need to be asked, perplexity corresponds to the number of equally likely choices that are available.[1]

The perplexity of a language model is related to the number of possible analyses for an expression. The grammatical model can be very tight, providing closely circumscribed coverage of sentences, and exhibiting low perplexity. On the other hand it can be less restricted, covering more types of syntactic constructions, but having a higher perplexity.

For example, suppose the language model M is a probabilistic finite state grammar network. Given a vocabulary $V = \{w_1, w_2, \ldots\}$ and states $S = \{s_1, s_2, \ldots\}$, the entropy at state s_i in the network is defined as follows:

$$H(M|s_i) = - \sum_{w_j \in V} P(w_j|s_i) \log P(w_j|s_i) \qquad (1.4)$$

The perplexity at state s is computed as follows:

$$Perplexity(M|s_i) = 2^{H(M|s_i)} \qquad (1.5)$$

The entropy of the entire network is computed as the sum of the entropies at the individual states, weighted by the probability of being in each state:

$$H(M) = \sum_{s_i} P(s_i) H(M|s_i) \qquad (1.6)$$

The perplexity of the language model is therefore defined as follows:

$$Perplexity = 2^{H(M)} \qquad (1.7)$$

A grammar that provides few constraints, where each word can be followed by many other words, would have a high entropy, and would exhibit high perplexity. A more restrictive grammar imposes more constraints, thereby reducing entropy and perplexity. Perplexity can be used directly to measure ambiguity, and we will use the terms "Residual Ambiguity" and the symbol "AMB" to denote it. For an example, please refer to Section 4.3.1.

1.2.2 Ambiguity Resolution Schemes

A "high-coverage" grammar with high perplexity provides more coverage, but results in higher degrees of ambiguity. This relationship holds for other knowledge sources used during analysis as well. For example, lexical knowledge sources (such as dictionaries and morphological analysis routines) that cover more forms cause higher lexical ambiguity.

An ambiguity resolution scheme requires an information source to determine which choices are more likely, and thereby helps to disambiguate

---

[1] It might be helpful to think of the game of twenty questions: Entropy measures how many questions need to be asked, while perplexity counts the number of possible objects.

the sentence analysis. Some ambiguity resolution schemes rely on elaborate knowledge sources. Experience has shown that strict syntactic constraints and semantic preference rules are difficult to scale up to wide-coverage parsing. Sources of semantic or pragmatic knowledge can require enormous effort to develop manually, and can prove difficult and slow to apply at parsing time. Thus, this type of disambiguating information is difficult to provide unless efficient knowledge acquisition and knowledge compilation methods can be found. Ambiguity resolution strategies that rely on the manual creation of constraints, rules, and domain models, as well as laborious hand-tuning, introduce a knowledge acquisition bottleneck. Furthermore, such methods are brittle if used beyond well-circumscribed domains. The purpose of this book is to describe a different approach that uses statistical learning to avoid this bottleneck.

1.3 Corpus-based Approaches to NLP

The "Chomskyan revolution" turned the attention of linguistics to models of grammar that are based on methods from formal language theory. But recently a new trend has emerged, often referred to as "corpus-based linguistics", which exhibits a number of different properties, as discussed below.

1.3.1 Empirical Orientation

Chomskyan linguistics posited an abstract notion of *language competence*, a pure formulation of speaker/hearer's knowledge about language, and about grammaticality versus ungrammaticality of sentences in particular. As in formal language theory, natural language was approached as a set of grammatical sentences.

In order to achieve expository and rhetorical aims, it is not uncommon for studies in this tradition to rely heavily on artificially-constructed, sometimes far-fetched natural language examples somewhere on the borderlines between grammatical, ungrammatical, and incomprehensible. This practice provides a striking contrast to the methodological orientation and empirical practice of corpus-based linguistics.

In corpus-based linguistics, attention is focussed on language *data*, as opposed to abstract models of grammatical competence. This has been fueled to no small extent by the recent availability of large text corpora, some of which are annotated with Part-of-Speech tags, phrase structure markers, and other types of analytic information.

One of the earliest projects in linguistic data collection was carried out by Francis and Kučera, who collected the Brown corpus. The Brown corpus consists of 1 million words of written American English that were published in the year 1961 [Francis and Kučera, 1982]. This work introduced the notion of Part-of-Speech (POS) tagging. POS tagging consists of annotating each word in a text with its Part-of-Speech. In the 1980s, a number of other corpus collection projects were started.

The Penn Treebank [Marcus et al., 1993] is a project at the University of Pennsylvania that collects, tags, brackets, and helps to disseminate online text corpora for research. There are now many collections of language data available; a good overview can be found in [Edwards, 1993]. See also [Armstrong, 1994] for examples of current research in corpus-based Approaches to natural language.

1.3.2 Naturally-Occurring Language

Corpus-based linguistics focuses on *naturally occurring* spoken and written language, as opposed to individual example sentences that are designed to illustrate specific points of grammatical theory. This is an important point that leads straight to the methodological heart of science. Science, as an empirical discipline, relies on data; first for inspection and speculation; then for model formulation; and finally for hypothesis testing, rejection, and model refinement.

Some grammatical theoreticians focus on the question of grammaticality of very specialized and rare syntactic constructions, and actually construct data aimed at particular problems which, along with grammaticality judgments, forms the data for their analyses. Corpus-based linguistics takes a different approach. Large corpora of naturally-occurring language are taken as the data that is to be accounted for. The immediate effect of this reorientation of the study of language is to divert attention away from the question of grammaticality, and towards the construction of models that can account for the diversity of language that is inevitably found in such corpora, falling liberally on both sides of the grammaticality rules from standard, prescriptive Grammar.

This desire to study naturally-occurring examples of actual language use is also reflected in the types of text and speech corpora that are being collected. The intent of the Brown corpus was to provide samples of all the major types of written English that were published in 1961. As is now realized, this was an overly ambitious goal, and today one would not claim such coverage for a corpus of such relatively small size. In fact, today's corpora are acknowledged to be "opportunistic" in nature — they provide whatever data can be obtained in the face of copyrights, restrictions arising out of concerns of confidentiality, proprietariness, etc. But the goal remains to document and account for the diversity and real-life use of language.

1.3.3 Emphasis on Evaluation

In the more applied strands of corpus-based research, an additional trend is visible: There is a significant concern with measuring performance and carrying out rigorous evaluations of natural language systems. Models are created to solve specific problems, and they are evaluated on realistic data. The models themselves are often probabilistic in nature, and they are trained by estimating model parameters from text corpora. The present work falls into this category. The key contributions to Natural Language Processing that is described in this work are a number of specific statistical models for the resolution of ambiguity arising from unknown words, Part-of-Speech ambiguity, and PP attachment. In each case, we carry out a rigorous evaluation, and compare the performance of our method to previously described work.

1.4 Statistical Modeling for Ambiguity Resolution

Ambiguity resolution is the biggest problem for robust natural language analysis. It has proven difficult to achieve robust language analysis using traditional approaches that rely on hand-coded syntactic constraints and domain-specific semantic and pragmatic rules for any large or open-ended domain.

Probabilistic models have the advantage of robustness, since they provide a measure of generalization beyond the training data, and usually exhibit graceful degradation. They allow for automatic training by means of model parameter estimation from text corpora. Thus, if adequate training data is available, the manual knowledge acquisition bottleneck can be avoided. However, current approaches employ relatively simple models of natural language ambiguity that are either limited to a single feature, or, if multiple features are used, that assume independence between the features.

This book presents a more powerful statistical approach to syntactic ambiguity resolution. It demonstrates that useful syntactic ambiguity resolution procedures can be trained automatically from large text corpora using the *loglinear* class of statistical models, which do not require any independence assumptions between the different features.

If appropriate training data are available, these models surpass simpler models in terms of measured performance on several ambiguity resolution tasks. And, unlike the knowledge-based approach, they require only the identification of potentially relevant features from the knowledge engineer.

1.5 Overview of this Book

The remainder of this book is structured as follows.

Chapter 2: Review. Chapter 2 presents a survey of previous work on syntactic ambiguity resolution, and summarizes their main advantages and shortcomings. It describes previous research on handling unknown words, and then traces the history of Part-of-Speech ambiguity resolution from the earliest approaches to the current favorite, stochastic Part-of-Speech tagging. Next, we describe syntactic, semantic, and pragmatic approaches to the problem of structural ambiguity. We pay particular attention to the problem of Prepositional Phrase attachment, and compare a number of recent corpus-based approaches to it.

Chapter 3: Theory. We take an approach to the problem of syntactic ambiguity resolution that is based on the loglinear model, a type of statistical model that is able to combine a number of categorical features. The advantage of using a loglinear model is that it takes into account the effects of combinations of feature values, as well as the main effects of individual feature values. The details of this approach, along with an example, are described in Chapter 3.

Chapter 4: Unknown Word Experiments. In the remainder of the book, we describe experiments concerning three types of ambiguity: modeling unknown words, Part-of-Speech ambiguity, and prepositional phrase attachment ambiguity. Chapter 4 concerns the modeling of unknown words. It shows that the loglinear model of unknown words obtains a higher accuracy than the probabilistic method described by [Weischedel et al., 1993], which assumes independence between the different features. On the same set of features, Weischedel at al. report 61% accuracy, while the loglinear method obtains 69% accuracy. When more features are added, the accuracy of the statistical model rises to 73%, while the performance of Weischedel et al.'s method degrades.

Chapter 5: POS Tagging Experiments. Chapter 5 concerns the resolution of Part-of-Speech ambiguity, or Part-of-Speech tagging. The experiments on Part-of-Speech ambiguity identify unknown words as an important source of error in Part-of-Speech tagging. We describe a baseline method that uses the prior distribution of infrequent words; this has a median accuracy on unknown words of 66%. The loglinear method raises the median accuracy to 80%. A simpler model of unknown words that assumes independence between the different features brings about significantly less improvement. An additional experiment on Part-of-Speech tagging with the statistical model results in a 19% reduction of tagging error on proper nouns, and a 4% reduction in overall tagging error.

Chapter 6: PP Attachment Experiments. A final set of experiments concerning Prepositional Phrase attachment ambiguity is described in Chapter 6. On the "Verb NP PP" pattern that has traditionally formed the subject of studies on automatic PP attachment, the loglinear method does not perform significantly better than the strategy of lexical association presented by [Hindle and Rooth, 1993]. The "Verb NP NP PP" pattern with three possible attachment sites, including two sites that have the same syntactic category, on the other hand, shows a marked improvement for the loglinear method. On this pattern, the lexical association strategy obtains a median accuracy of 72%, while the loglinear method raises the median accuracy to 79%.

Chapter 7: Conclusions. Chapter 7 summarizes the results and contributions of this work, and points out some possible areas for future research.

Appendices. The appendices provide a number of foundational and technical details on entropy, the tagset, the procedure for obtaining random samples, the confusion matrices from our Part-of-Speech tagging experiments, methods for massaging the corpus, and on the interface between our COMMON LISP programs and the statistical modeling package S-PLUS.

2. Previous Work on Syntactic Ambiguity Resolution

Syntactic ambiguity has been studied from a number of perspectives. Previous work has described syntactic, semantic, and pragmatic principles, as well some corpus-based methods, for ambiguity resolution. This chapter surveys the main results, and summarizes the strengths and shortcomings of previous approaches.

2.1 A Note on Reported Error Rates

In much of the literature that reports experimental results of corpus-based NLP methods, the performance of different methods is summarized as a single mean accuracy figure. This figure represent the accuracy to which a given method will converge if it is repeated a large number of times. The mean accuracy is usually reported with a precision of one, and sometimes even two, decimal points. In this review, the policy is simply to repeat the accuracy figures as stated in the literature. However, it should be noted that it is probably not meaningful to report results to such a high degree of precision. Furthermore, when different methods are compared, it is not clear what represents a statistically significant difference. This depends on the error distribution for the techniques being compared (which is usually not known), and on the number and size of the samples. An intuitive way of displaying and comparing results is to take a large number of samples from a pool of previously unseen evaluation data, and graphing the results using boxplots. This is the approach adopted in this work; see Section 5.3.3 for further details.

2.2 The Problem of Unknown Words

Words can be divided into two kinds: Words that fall into open classes, and words that fall into closed classes. An open class is a word class whose membership is indefinite, and which increases as new concepts are added to the language; this includes nouns, verbs, and adjectives. A closed word class is rarely extended, and contains a relatively small number of high-frequency words. The closed word classes include pronouns, determiners, prepositions, and the like.

While it is possible to list all of the closed class words in the lexicon, open class words can never be covered entirely. There are simply too many of them; every technical discipline, for example, has its own large set of domain-specific terminology.

To illustrate this point, suppose a parser is applied to text from a newswire. Some of the unknown words it might encounter are shown in the following list, which was created by looking at a Wall Street Journal article: *Pierre Vinken, crocidolite, asbestos-related, mesothelioma*. Unless a parser is applied to a highly circumscribed domain, it must include a mechanism to handle unknown words.

2.2.1 AI Approaches to Unknown Words

Early work on handling unknown words was performed in the framework of conceptual parsing [Schank, 1975], [Schank and Abelson, 1977]. Conceptual parsing uses syntactic, semantic, and pragmatic information to guide parsing. This information can be used to guess properties of new words. [Granger, 1977] and [Carbonell, 1979] describe the "project and integrate" method — project all constraints from the syntactic and semantic analysis of the surrounding text onto the unknown words, and then integrate the constraints with each other and the context to derive a characterization of the unknown word. [Carbonell, 1979] also described a simple truth maintenance method that allowed retraction of inferences that later proved contradictory. This method, however, required a sufficient domain model to restrict the ambiguity of the interpretation of the known part of the sentence.

2.2.2 Morphological Analysis of Unknown Words

Morphological analysis can also provide some clues about the syntactic category of unknown words. [Black, 1991] describes some work where morphological analysis of new words was used in order to handle new words for a speech generation application. However, morphological analysis is not sufficient to solve the problem of new words entirely, because there is morphological ambiguity. Consider the following two examples:

a. We looked at the <u>ducks</u>. (waterfowl)   (2.1)
b. When they throw rotten eggs at the singer, he just <u>ducks</u>.

The word *ducks* is ambiguous between a noun and a verb interpretation, even though the word carries category-specific inflection in both cases: The noun carries the "plural' inflection, and the verb carries the "third person singular" suffix, but these two suffixes are identical in English. (See Chapter 5 for a discussion of Part-of-Speech tagging, which currently provides the most effective solution to this problem.)

2.2.3 Corpus-based Approaches to Unknown Words

[Weischedel et al., 1993] describe the POST system for Part-of-Speech (POS) tagging, which includes a probabilistic model for unknown words. The authors report an error rate of about 50% for trigram-based unknown word tagging, where an unknown word could fall into one of 22 open class POSs. When the authors added a model of two morphological word features, inflectional ending and derivational ending, the error rate fell to about 18%. Adding model parameters for capitalization further reduced the error rate to 15%.

The PEARL system [Magerman and Marcus, 1991] is a chart parser that combines Ken Church's trigram-based POS tagger, a probabilistic unknown word model, and a probabilistic grammar. In PEARL, unknown words are assumed to be in one of the open class categories, with a probability function that mirrors the distribution of the open classes in the training corpus. For example, if 40% of the open-class words in the training data were nouns, than an unknown word would be assigned a 40% probability of being a noun.

2.3 Lexical Syntactic Ambiguity

Many words can belong to more than one syntactic category or Part-of-Speech (POS). In fact, examining the Brown corpus confirms the suspicion that most open class words can be used as nouns, verbs, or adjectives [Church, 1988]. The process of resolving lexical syntactic ambiguity and annotating each word in a sentence with a POS label or *tag* has come to be called *Part-of-Speech tagging*, or POS tagging for short.

The following sections cite accuracy results as they were reported by the authors. Care must be taken in evaluating the performance of different approaches. The difficulty of the tagging problem depends on the nature and degree of homogeneity of the training and evaluation corpora, the number of tags in the tagset, and a number of other factors. Without a standardized POS tagging evaluation corpus, or a way to quantify and compensate for these variations, these accuracy figures can not necessarily be compared directly to each other in a meaningful way.

2.3.1 Rule-based Lexical Syntactic Ambiguity Resolution

[Klein and Simmons, 1963] described one of the earliest rule-based POS taggers. Subsequently, [Green and Rubin, 1971] created the TAGGIT tagging program for tagging the Brown corpus. The process is divided into two stages: *Initial tag selection* identifies all possible tags for a word, and *tag disambiguation* chooses the most appropriate tag.

Tag selection in TAGGIT is performed as follows. First, lexical items are looked up in an "exception dictionary" of about 3,000 entries. The dictionary includes most closed-class words. Next, TAGGIT handles a list of special cases, such as contractions, special symbols, and capitalized words. Finally, the word is checked against a suffix list with approximately 450 entries. As a default, a word is assigned the three tags for "noun, verb, adjective".

Tag disambiguation in TAGGIT is based on manually-created heuristic rules which use a word's local context to determine the correct POS. TAGGIT incorporates 3,300 "context frame rules" that depend on up to two words before and after the target word. The general form of these rules and an example is shown below, where "?" indicates the tag to be disambiguated:

$$\text{tag}_i \ \text{tag}_j \ ? \ \text{tag}_k \ \text{tag}_l \ \longrightarrow \ \text{result-tag}$$
$$\text{tag}_i \ \text{tag}_j \ ? \ \text{tag}_k \ \text{tag}_l \ \longrightarrow \ \text{not tag}$$

An example of a TAGGIT rule is shown below. The rule states that a word preceding a third person singular verb (which is tagged VBZ) can not be a plural noun (NNS).

$$? \ \text{VBZ} \ \longrightarrow \ \text{not NNS}$$

Considerable effort went into creating, debugging, and refining the TAGGIT rules. TAGGIT employed 86 basic tags, and a tagging accuracy of 77% of the words was reported by [Francis and Kučera, 1982]. The tagging of the entire Brown corpus was completed manually by correcting the remaining errors.

2.3.2 Frequency-based POS Tagging

[Garside et al., 1987] reports work that is based on the Lancaster-Oslo-Bergen (LOB) corpus of written British English. The LOB corpus mirrors the makeup and coverage of the Brown corpus for modern British English.

The LOB corpus tagging program is called the "Constituent-Likelihood Automatic Word-Tagging System", or CLAWS. CLAWS uses 130 different Parts-of-Speech. Its dictionary is based on the tagged Brown corpus, and it contains about 7,000 entries. The suffix list has about 700 entries.

A bigram is a pair of POS labels, such as ¡Determiner,Noun¿. The procedure for tag disambiguation in CLAWS was designed in response to the important observation that about 80% of the attempted applications of TAGGIT rules concerned rules that only made reference to the immediately following or preceding word. In other words, 80% of rule applications in TAGGIT concerned only bigrams. Based on this, CLAWS was designed to use a "matrix of collocational possibilities", a precursor to today's bigram probabilities.

Bigram probabilities in CLAWS are estimated using Maximum Likelihood (ML) estimates[1] based on bigram frequencies in "a large proportion of the tagged Brown corpus." Initially, the following formula was used for bigram

---

[1] Maximum Likelihood (ML) estimates for model parameters refer to the estimates that maximize the *likelihood function* for the sampling scheme. The likelihood function is a function of the parameters to the probability of the observed samples. Thus, given a particular sampling scheme, the ML estimates for the

probabilities, where t_i denote POS tags, and $f(t_i)$ denotes the observed frequency of tag t_i:

$$P(t_i, t_{i+1}) \approx \frac{f(t_i, t_{i+1})}{f(t_i)} \tag{2.2}$$

However, this was found to favor high-frequency tags too much, and the following definition was adopted instead:

$$P(t_i, t_{i+1}) \approx \frac{f(t_i, t_{i+1})}{f(t_i)f(t_{i+1})} \tag{2.3}$$

The probabilities were smoothed with a small floor to avoid ruling out tag sequences when a bigram was not observed due to sparse data.

Tag sequences were disambiguated in the following way. Consider an ambiguous tag sequence of length n. This defines a number of possible disambiguated tag sequences, $T_1, T_2, \ldots, T_k$. The value of a tag sequence T_j, $V(T_j)$, is defined as the product of the probabilities of the bigrams in the sequence:

$$V(T) = \prod_{i=1}^{n-1} P(t_i, t_{i+1}) \tag{2.4}$$

CLAWS uses token-based tagging. The probability of a tag sequence T_j was estimated as the value of the sequence divided by the sum of the values of all possible sequences:

$$P(T_j) \approx \frac{val(T_j)}{\sum_{i=1}^{k} val(T_i)} \tag{2.5}$$

CLAWS uses a measure of "relative tag probabilities" to take into account the likelihood of a tag, given a word. This is not achieved by statistical estimation of probabilities, but rather by using two markers in the dictionary indicating "less than 1 in 10 cases" and "less than 1 in 100 cases."

Further extensions to improve performance include the incorporation of a number of trigram-based scaling factors. For example, the trigram (¡be¿ ¡adverb¿ ¡past-tense-verb¿) is assigned a scaling factor that decreases the probability of a tag sequence containing it in comparison to a tag sequence containing the trigram (¡be¿ ¡adverb¿ ¡past-participle/adjective¿). This expresses the notion that after a form of the verb to be, a past participle or an adjective is more likeli than a past tense verb. A similar scheme is employed for conjunctions, where tag associations hold across the conjunction. A module called IDIOMTAG, intervening between tag selection and tag disambiguation, was added to handle multi-word sequences. IDIOMTAG accounts

---

parameters are those values that give the observed data the highest probability of occurrence. In practice, the sampling scheme in corpus-based language modeling is usually not stated, but implicitly assumed to be multinomial. Given a multinomial sampling scheme, it can be shown that proportions based directly on observed frequencies yield ML estimates.

for approximately 1% of text tokens [DeRose, 1988]. Some examples of the application of IDIOMTAG are shown below.

in order that, tagged as a subordinating conjunction
so that, tagged as a subordinating conjunction
so as to, tagged as infinitival *to*

CLAWS is reported to be 96%–97% accurate on the entire LOB corpus, using the bigram probabilities along with a few trigram exceptions as described above. Without IDIOMTAG, about 94% accuracy was achieved on a 15,000 word sample.

2.3.3 Hidden Markov Models for Lexical Disambiguation

[Kupiec, 1992] describes an alternative approach that is based on a Hidden Markov Model (HMM). An HMM is a mathematical model of a stochastic process, defined as a collection of states connected by transitions. Movement through the transition network occurs according to a probabilistic transition function. Symbols are emitted when an arc is traversed. This occurs according to a second probabilistic function, the output function which defines the conditional probability of emitting a symbol given that a certain transition is taken. An HMM for tagging can be trained from an untagged corpus; a lexicon describing the possible tags for words is required, however.

In the initial model, there is one state for each POS category. The topology of the HMM is a fully interconnected network. Words are emitted as arcs are traversed, but since there are so many words, it is infeasible to estimate parameters for every single word on every arc. Instead, Kupiec divided words into different classes depending on their possible POS tags. There were 129 such "word equivalence classes". With additional classes for the most common words, there were about 400 classes. The progression from POS to POS is modeled by progressing along the HMM states, and words are generated according to the arcs' output functions.

The training corpus was over 1 million words of electronic mail about the design of the Common Lisp programming language. Kupiec also describes improvements to this basic model. More POS categories were added; individual equivalence classes were created for the 100 most frequent words; the Markov network was manually edited in some places; and the topology of the network was extended to a higher-order model in selected places that were responsible for a lot of errors.

Kupiec reports the following results from his basic model (the first-order network): With a closed dictionary (estimated directly from the corpus), training on 440,000 words from the Brown corpus, and testing on 440,000 words from the Brown corpus: 95.7% overall accuracy, and 88.2% accuracy on ambiguous words. With an open dictionary (there were about 3% unknown words in the training text), training on 70,000-110,000 words of "humor columnist" material, and testing on 440,000 words from the Brown corpus, the overall accuracy was 94.7%, and the accuracy on ambiguous words was 85.2%. Extending the network provided an improvement of 0.6% for ambiguous words.

[Cutting et al., 1992] also describe an HMM-based tagging system. The Forward-Backward algorithm [Baum, 1972] is used to estimate the HMM parameters, and the Viterbi algorithm [Viterbi, 1967] is used for tagging. The authors describe how the HMM can be tuned: Equivalence classes (ambiguity classes) can be manually annotated with favored tags, and states can be manually annotated with favored transitions. This is achieved by setting the disfavored probabilities to a small constant, and redistributing the remaining probability mass to the other possibilities. With a lexicon constructed from the Brown Corpus, training on one half of the corpus, and tagging the other half, 96% accuracy was achieved.

[Schuetze and Singer, 1994] describe an approach to POS tagging that uses HMMs with variable length histories. The history lengths are adjusted automatically based on the training data. An accuracy of 95.81% is reported. For a summary of reported overall error rates, and error rates on unknown words, see also Table 5.2 and Table 5.1.

2.3.4 N-Gram based Stochastic POS Tagging

Just as most of TAGGIT's rules concern bigrams. [Church, 1988] notes a similar effect with Donald Hindle's FIDDITCH parser [Hindle, 1983]. FIDDITCH is a deterministic Marcus-style parser with very wide coverage. Many of the disambiguation rules in FIDDITCH can be reformulated in terms of bigram and trigram probabilities. Automatically estimating such probabilities could be easier than manually creating, testing, and debugging symbolic disambiguation heuristics.

[Church, 1988] describes the PARTS POS tagger that implements such a model. A POS tag is assigned to the current word based partly on the POS tags of the next two words. Two sets of parameters are used:

- **Lexical Probabilities:** $P(t|w)$ — the probability of observing tag t given that word w occurred.
- **Contextual Probabilities:** $P(t_i|t_{i+1}, t_{i+2})$ — the probability of observing tag t_i given that the two following tags t_{i+1} and t_{i+2} have occurred.

The probabilities were estimated from the tagged Brown corpus using Maximum Likelihood estimation as follows:

- **Lexical Probability:** $P(t|w) \approx \frac{f(t,w)}{f(w)}$, where $f(t, w)$ is the frequency of observing word w with tag t.
- **Contextual Probability:** $P(t_i|t_{i+1}, t_{i+2}) \approx \frac{f(t_i, t_{i+1}, t_{i+2})}{f(t_{i+1}, t_{i+2})}$

Probabilities are smoothed by adding 1 to the frequency counts $f(t|w)$ based on the POS assigned to words in a machine-readable dictionary, and by making the necessary adjustment to $f(w)$. This allows tag assignments that were not observed in the corpus because of sparse data. Further smoothing was performed by discarding low-frequency capitalized nouns, which appear because the Brown corpus includes misleadingly capitalized words from titles.

Church's POS tagger uses the Viterbi algorithm to find POS tags that maximize the product of the lexical probability and the contextual probability. The algorithm's complexity is linear in the number of words in the sentence. Given an input sentence of length n (assuming padding with two "end-of-sentence" markers), the POS assignment is chosen that maximizes the following quantity:

$$\prod_{i=1}^{n} P(t_i|w_i)P(t_i|t_{i+1}, t_{i+2}) \tag{2.6}$$

The algorithm is $O(n)$ because it takes advantage of the fact that this is a second order Markov model, and so only limited context is taken into account. Church uses forward tag context, and his algorithm works backwards from the last word to the first word in the sentence. Given a window of three words, a partial tag sequence $t_1t_2t_x \ldots$ can be discarded if there is any other partial tag sequence $t_1t_2t_y \ldots$ such that the second sequence has a higher score. The reason for this is that all further score will depend only on t_1t_2, which are the same for both sequences. Since t_x is past the window of three, no further tags can raise the score.

The effect is to limit the number of paths that need to be considered to a polynomial of the number of available tags. To be precise, for an n-th order Markov model with tagset $T = \{t_1, t_2, \ldots, t_n\}$ the upper bound on this number is $|T|^n$. For a large tagset this seems high, but in practice many tag pairs do not occur. Furthermore, beam search can be employed to further limit the number of active paths by only keeping the partial paths above a certain threshold score, and discarding all other partial paths.

[DeRose, 1988] also describes the use of a dynamic programming algorithm for POS tagging which uses path-based tagging. In his system, called VOLSUNGA, 97 tags are used. DeRose contrasts his work with CLAWS, the LOB tagger described in Section 2.3.2 above. VOLSUNGA uses bigrams and no idiom tagging, and achieves 96% word accuracy. VOLSUNGA includes no unknown word handling -- all words are listed in the lexicon. Furthermore, VOLSUNGA's parameters are estimated from the entire Brown corpus.

DeRose notices that the number of paths retained at any stage during tagging is "the degree of ambiguity at that stage", which should be much smaller than the upper bound $|T|^n$ that was shown above. Only about 3,900 of 9,409 theoretically possible tag pairs occur in the Brown corpus, Thus, the actual POS entropy (and hence ambiguity) is much lower than the upper bound.

2.4 Structural Ambiguity

The syntactic structure of a sentence indicates how the parts of the sentence should be combined during interpretation, just as the syntactic structure of an arithmetic expression or of a computer program determines its meaning. When more than one syntactic structure could be assigned to a given sentence, the sentence is structurally ambiguous. This section surveys previous approaches to the resolution of structural ambiguity.

2.4.1 Syntactic Approaches

Syntactic approaches to ambiguity resolution use *structural properties* of the parse tree to choose a particular parse. [Bever, 1970] formulated a number of heuristics for syntactic ambiguity resolution. Consider the following example:

– **Strategy B** or **Canonical Sentoid Strategy.** The first N... V... (N)... clause is the main clause, unless the verb is marked as subordinate.

Bever's "Strategy B" rule would be used to account for the *garden-path* effect in some sentences. In a garden-path sentence, the reader begins to interpret the sentence in accordance with the canonical sentoid strategy, but the correct interpretation turns out to be a different interpretation, and the reader needs to make an effort (often conscious) to re-interpret the sentence. Consider the famous garden path sentence:

The horse raced past the barn fell.   (2.7)

Most readers interpret the sequence *raced past the barn* as the verb phrase of the main sentence when they first read the sentence, but actually it is a reduced relative clause that attaches to the subject *the horse*. The correct interpretation can be paraphrased as *The horse that was raced past the barn fell (to the ground)*.

[Kimball, 1973] presented a set of principles of human parsing mechanisms. Some of these principles contained prescriptions concerning the resolution of structural ambiguity:

– **Right Association.** Terminal symbols (lexical categories) aim to attach to the lowest right non-terminal node in the parse tree.
– **Two Sentence Memory Limit.** "The constituents of no more than two sentences can be parsed at the same time."
– **Early Closure.** A phrase is closed as soon as possible (no further attachment is allowed to that phrasal node), "unless the next node parsed is an immediate constituent of that phrase."
– **Backtracking is Expensive.** When a phrase has been closed, it is "costly in terms of perceptual complexity" to backtrack and reorganize the constituents of that phrase.

Building on Kimball's work, [Frazier, 1979] and [Frazier and Fodor, 1978] proposed the following two principles of human parse preference:

- **Minimal Attachment.** Do not postulate any unnecessary nodes in the parse tree.
- **Late Closure.** If grammatically permissible, attach new items into the clause or phrase currently being processed (i.e. the phrase or clause postulated most recently).

These two principles are ordered, so that Minimal Attachment determines sentence structure if the two rules are in conflict.

[Gibson, 1991] presents a theory of human parsing that addresses garden-path effects, preferred interpretations for ambiguous input, and a number of other psycholinguistic effects. Gibson's parsing framework assumes a cost scheme where lexical, syntactic, and thematic properties of a partial parse incur certain costs, which are combined in a linear equation to form a total cost. An overall ceiling on "cognitive load" as measured by total cost is imposed. Multiple structures are kept during parsing if their cost is similar; if one partial parse is significantly more costly, it is discarded. Gibson uses three properties for cost assignment:

- **Thematic Reception.** A constituent that needs to fill a thematic role, but which does not know whose thematic role it fills (it does not know its θ-assigner) causes a certain cost.
- **Lexical Requirement.** A construction that has certain lexical requirements, but which does not have the requisite fillers, causes a certain cost.
- **Recency Preference.** Local attachment is preferred over attachment to more distant nodes. This principle is closely related to Kimball's principle of Right Attachment, and Frazier's principle of Late Closure.

[Ford et al., 1982] describe the principle of "lexical preference". This principle may be paraphrased as follows:

- **Lexical Preference.** Give priority to the interpretations that are consistent with the strongest lexical form of the predicate.

Ford et al. state that the stronger or preferred forms are those that occur with higher frequency. This has clear relevance to any statistical approach. For further discussion of this approach from the perspective of human sentence processing, see [Trueswell et al., 1994] and [Frazier, 1987].

2.4.2 Semantic Approaches

Not all cases of syntactic ambiguity can be resolved with reference to syntactic properties of the sentence alone, so there has been a significant amount of work on semantic features for disambiguation. The "selectional restrictions" of [Katz and Fodor, 1963] are an early example. Katz and Fodor's selectional restrictions were phrased in terms of semantic binary features, such as

ANIMATE; they provided constraints on syntactic roles, such as arguments of verbs.

Much of the work that uses semantic rules to perform disambiguation can be traced back to the framework of conceptual parsing [Schank, 1975], [Schank and Abelson, 1977]. Parsing systems that fall into this paradigm include case-frame parsers [Carbonell and Hayes, 1987], and expectation-driven parsing [Riesbeck, 1987]. These parsers used domain-specific semantic knowledge to drive the parsing process, and to perform disambiguation.

The model of *Naive Semantics* presented by [Dahlgren, 1988] is a system of commonsense semantic interpretation based on conceptual primitives. An elaborate model of domain and commonsense knowledge is used for disambiguation. PP attachment is performed using three types of knowledge:

- **Lexical level commonsense heuristics.** This includes rules of the form "If the prepositional object is temporal, then the PP modifies the sentence."
- **Lexical knowledge.** An example of a syntactic disambiguation rule is "certain intransitive verbs require certain prepositions, e.g. *depend on, look for.*"
- **Preposition-specific rules.** An example of a preposition-specific rule is, "if the preposition is the word *at*, and the prepositional object is abstract or the prepositional object is a place, then attach the PP to the sentence. Otherwise, attach it to the NP."

Dahlgren uses a "commonsense world model" that provides ontological concepts like TEMPORAL and PLACE. Ambiguity resolution procedures can use the notion of "ontological similarity", essentially meaning reasonable closeness in the type hierarchy.

Another example of an NLP system that uses semantic rules for disambiguation is the KBMT-89 machine translation system, which is described in [Goodman and Nirenburg, 1991]. In this system, semantic case-frame representations are built up in tandem with the syntactic parse tree. Various semantic restrictions are placed on semantic role-fillers in the case-frames. An ontology provides a hierarchy of semantic primitives, which can be used to perform limited types of semantic inference about potential semantic role-fillers.

Graeme Hirst's ABSITY system for parsing and semantic interpretation [Hirst, 1986] also uses semantic selectional restrictions for disambiguation. The semantic knowledge is represented as a semantic net, implemented as an inheritance hierarchy of frames. ABSITY uses a mechanism called the "Semantic Enquiry Desk" for syntactic disambiguation, which includes attachment decisions. Hirst employs a frame-based representation system losely based on Montague's higher order intensional logic. In making attachment decisions, the Semantic Enquiry Desk implements the following semantic principles:

- **Verb-guided Preferences.** An attachment is favored if it obeys verb-guided preferences, as stated in the case slots of the frame corresponding to the verb. Cases may be "compulsory", "preferred", or "unpreferred". This implements the lexical preference strategy of [Ford et al., 1982].
- **Semantic Plausibility.** An attachment is preferred if it is plausible. Plausibility is determined by "slot restriction predicates", a somewhat refined notion of selectional restrictions.
- **Pragmatic Plausibility.** Following the "Exemplar Principle", ABSITY also considers objects or actions plausible if "the knowledge base contains an instance of such an object or action, or an instance of something similar." This implements the pragmatic principles of [Crain and Steedman, 1985].

In general, it is a common characteristic of these systems that a large amount of elaborate semantic knowledge is needed. Given this knowledge, effective strategies for dealing with unusual and extragrammatical input can be implemented [Carbonell and Hayes, 1984], [Carbonell and Hayes, 1983].

It should be pointed out that it is clear that semantic rules are necessary to resolve difficult cases of ambiguity. Such difficult cases may involve unusual semantic relations in the sentence. For example, consider the problem of word-sense ambiguity in a sentence that contains an instance of metonymy[2] [Fass, 1988]:

$$\text{Mary drank the glasses.} \qquad (2.8)$$

In order to determine the correct sense of the noun *glasses* ("drinking vessel" or "spectacles") some semantic inferencing has to be performed. Thus, in the limit, ambiguity resolution requires semantic knowledge.

2.4.3 Pragmatic Approaches

Pragmatics is the study of language use, and of the role of language in communication and social interaction. Crain and Steedman [Crain and Steedman, 1985] propose a number of pragmatic principles to account for parse preferences:

- **A Priori Plausibility.** If an interpretation is more plausible in terms either of general knowledge about the world, or of specific knowledge about the universe of discourse, then, everything else being equal, it is favored over an interpretation that is not as plausible.
- **Referential Success.** If an interpretation refers to an entity already established in the discourse model that is being constructed by the hearer, then it is preferred over an interpretation that does not refer to such a known entity.
- **Parsimony.** If an interpretation carries fewer unconfirmed (but consistent) presuppositions or entailments, then, everything else being equal,

---

[2] "Metonymy is a nonliteral figure of speech in which the name of one thing is substituted for that of another related to it." [Fass, 1988]

that interpretation is adopted, and the presuppositions are incorporated into the discourse model. Note that the principle of Referential Success is a special case of this principle.

In order to apply these principles, disambiguation is performed by making choices based on an evolving discourse model and on general world knowledge. Again, it is likely that some cases of ambiguity can only be resolved on the basis of such pragmatic principles. At the same time, pragmatic rules of this nature presuppose elaborate domain and world models, which makes them difficult to implement in a parsing system.

2.5 Prepositional Phrase Attachment Disambiguation

Prepositional phrases (PPs) are one of the most frequent sources of structural ambiguity. English PPs typically occur towards the end of the sentence, which allows them to attach to most of the preceding constituents of the sentence.

This is an important point. All recent corpus-based studies of PP attachment disambiguation have limited their attention to the problem of a PP with only two possible attachment sites, a verb and a noun phrase. As suggested by [Gibson and Pearlmutter, 1994] and discussed further in Chapter 6, this oversimplification results in a distorted picture of the PP attachment problem, and makes it look easier than it actually is.

Many PPs are not limited to just two possible attachment sites that differ in syntactic category. To illustrate this point, here are some examples showing some different possible attachments sites for English PPs:[3]

- **Right Association: Attachment to most recent NP.** A PP can attach to the most recent NP. An example is shown in Figure 2.1, where the PP *of the tube* attaches to the NP *the surface*.
- **Minimal Attachment: Attachment to VP.** A PP attached to the VP modifies the entire verb phrase. An example is shown in Figure 2.2, where the PP *with the supplied instrument* attaches at the level of the VP.
- **Attachment to a higher NP.** A PP can also attach to a higher NP, i.e. an NP that dominates (is above) the most recent NP in the parse tree. (Crossing attachments are usually not possible.) An example is shown in Figure 2.3, where the PP *under normal load* attaches to the higher NP node and thus modifies the NP *the signal strength*.
- **Attachment to an Adjectival Phrase.** In some cases, a PP can also attach to an adjectival phrase. This is illustrated in Figure 2.4, where the PP *to the unit* is attached to the adjective *harmful*. Compare this to Figure 2.5, where the PP *after extensive testing* skips over the adjective, and instead attaches to the VP.

---

[3] The parse trees in this document were generated using Kevin Knight's TREEPRINT package [Knight, 1987].

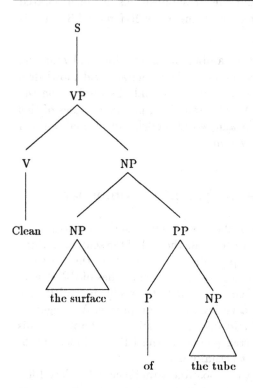

Fig. 2.1. PP Attachment to Most Recent NP

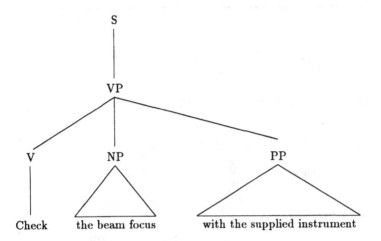

Fig. 2.2. PP Attachment to VP

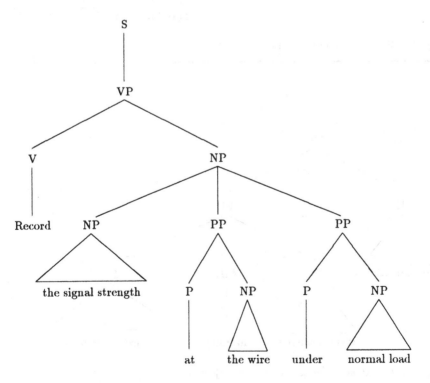

Fig. 2.3. PP Attachment to Higher NP

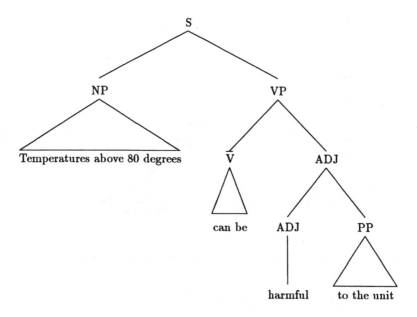

Fig. 2.4. PP Attachment to Adjective

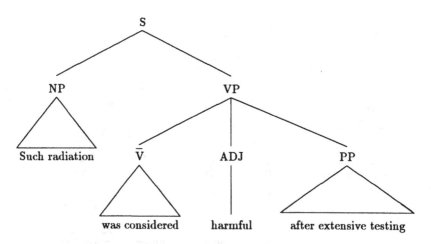

Fig. 2.5. PP Attachment to VP Above Adjective

As has been noted in the literature, PP attachment ambiguity is compounded if a sentence contains multiple PPs. Consider the following examples, again from a technical manual:

This voltage is measured <u>at the MVP point</u>   (2.9)
<u>in the memory circuit</u>
<u>below the adjustment unit.</u>

There are three PPs, and the attachment ambiguities multiply. Each PP can attach to the VP, or to the NPs of the previous PPs, as long as there are no crossed attachments in the parse tree.

2.5.1 Using Lexical Associations for PP Attachment Disambiguation

[Ford et al., 1982] introduced the notion of *lexical preferences* for ambiguity resolution, and [Hindle and Rooth, 1993] described a method for learning lexical association strengths for PP attachment from a text corpus. Like all other recent corpus-based studies, Hindle & Rooth only addressed the pattern of a verb followed by a noun phrase and a PP. The problem was further simplified by only considering the head words of the constituents:

$[_{Verb}$ Adjust] the beam $[_{Noun_1}$ focus] $[_{Preposition}$ with]   (2.10)
the calibration $[_{Noun_2}$ tool].

The lexical association strengths were estimated statistically from a training corpus. The training corpus consisted of 13 million words of 1989 AP newswire stories. The texts were tagged by Church's POS tagger, and then parsed by Hindle's FIDDITCH parser. This yielded 2.6 million NPs. From the parsed text, a table containing 223,666 verb–noun–preposition triples was extracted.

The table of verb–noun–preposition triples summarizes occurrences of PPs with attachment ambiguity. PPs in these triples are assigned to nouns or verbs according to a set of heuristics. This results in a set of attachment "bigrams". Then, Maximum Likelihood estimates were used to derive the following probabilities:

$P_{verb-attach}$(preposition— verb,noun)
$P_{noun-attach}$(preposition— verb,noun)

The probabilities for specific nouns and verbs were smoothed with each preposition's observed frequency of noun attachment and verb attachment in general, $\frac{f(N,p)}{f(N)}$ and $\frac{f(V,p)}{f(V)}$. The attachment decision was then based on the log likelihood ratio between the probabilities for verb and noun attachment.

The results on a test set of 880 verb-noun-preposition triples from the AP newswire are summarized in Table 2.1. The gold standard was defined as the set of attachments on which a number of experts agreed. Of the correct attachments for this set, 586 (67%) are to the noun, and 294 (33%) to the verb. The automatic lexical association procedure had an average accuracy rate of approximately 80%.

Table 2.1. Results of Hindle & Rooth

Attachment Method	Accuracy
Right Association (noun)	67%
Minimal Attachment (verb)	33%
Human Judges using triples only	85%-88%
Automatic Attachment	80%

These results were analyzed, and the authors determined that their strategy worked well on attaching arguments to nouns and verbs (nouns: 88.5% accuracy, verbs: 86.4% accuracy); worse on attaching adjuncts, such as time and manner phrases (nouns: 72.5% accuracy, verbs: 61.3% accuracy), and worse yet on idioms and other types of PPs (61%-65% accuracy).

2.5.2 Systematic Ambiguity in PP Attachment

It is not always possible to identify a single, correct attachment. This should be taken into account when evaluating automatic attachment procedures. Hindle and Rooth identified a number of such patterns:

- **Phrasal Verbs and Idioms.** Phrasal verbs and idioms may include "spurious nouns" that cannot function as PP attachment sites. Example: *... take place in the city.*
- **Light Verbs.** In a light verb construction, the verb has a relatively low semantic content, and it is not clear what the proper PP attachment should be. Example: *... make cuts in Social Security.*
- **Systematic Locative Ambiguity.** If an action is performed involving an object in a place, then both the action and the object are in the place. Where should the locative PP attach? Example: *... visit sights in Seattle.*
- **Systematic Benefactive Ambiguity.** If something is arranged for someone, then the thing arranged is also for them. Where should the benefactive PP attach? Example: *... prepare a summary for him.*
- **Other Systematic PP Attachment Ambiguities.** In many other cases, it is difficult to identify a semantic difference between attachments because both interpretations seem to entail each other.

2.5.3 PP Attachment and Class-based Generalization

Hindle and Rooth's work estimated lexical association strengths between verbs/nouns and prepositions, so their sample space consisted of the cross-product of the set of nouns/verbs and the set of prepositions. It seems intuitively plausible that the objects of the PPs contain some disambiguating information, but adding the PP objects would mean enlarging the sample space to the cross-product of the set of verbs/nouns, the set of prepositions, and the set of nouns. Hindle & Rooth's lexically-based probability estimation scheme would not work over such a large sample space. Two subsequent studies solved this problem by coarsening the sample space by grouping words together into word classes.

[Resnik and Hearst, 1993] describe a series of experiments that included the prepositional objects. The nominal synonym sets from WORDNET were used to provide the word classes. Both the attachment site and the prepositional object are placed into a semantic or *conceptual* class, and the relative strengths of the *conceptual association* between the classes via the preposition were estimated from a text corpus.

Resnik & Hearst used the parsed Wall Street Journal (WSJ) texts from the Penn Treebank [Marcus et al., 1993]. The model was evaluated on 174 test cases. Hindle & Rooth's lexical association strategy on this data achieved 81.6% accuracy, while Resnik & Hearst's conceptual association strategy obtained an average accuracy of 77.6%. The two methods were combined by choosing the conceptual strategy if its confidence was above a threshold, and else the lexical association strategy. Under this scheme, overall accuracy was 82.2%.

2.5.4 A Maximum Entropy Model of PP Attachment

[Ratnaparkhi et al., 1994] report another study that used class-based generalization. In this experiment, the classes were derived automatically with a Mutual Information clustering procedure [Brown et al., 1990]. The method used features that correspond to exact word matching on any of the four head words (Verb, $Noun_1$, Preposition, $Noun_2$), and class membership of a head word.

An automatic procedure was used to select the most informative subset of all the possible features; peak performance was obtained with around 200 features. These features were combined in a Maximum Entropy model. Using the parsed WSJ corpus, trained on 20,000 PP cases, and evaluated on 3,000 cases, the model achieved 81.6% accuracy. A second experiment was performed on IBM Computer Manuals that were annotated by the University of Lancaster. Here, after training on 8,000 PP cases, an evaluation on 900 PP cases showed 84.1% accuracy.

Ratnaparkhi et al. compared their maximum entropy method to decision trees using the same features, and found that the decision tree procedure had lower accuracy: 77.7% on WSJ texts, and 79.5% on the Computer Manuals. They also reported the results of some experiments involving humans experts. Judged against the WSJ corpus, a human treebanking expert that only saw the four head words performed at 88.2%; if shown the whole sentence, the human accuracy rose to 93.2%. (Recall that the gold standard was the set of attachments on which a set of treebanking experts agreed.)

2.5.5 Learning Symbolic PP Attachment Rules

[Brill and Resnik, 1994] described some experiments in Brill's framework of Transformation-based learning. First, an initial annotation is performed; in the case of PP attachment, all PPs are attached to the noun. Second, the procedure iterates through comparing the current annotations to the correct annotations in the corpus, and learns transformations that improve the accuracy.

The method employs a greedy learning algorithm. At every iteration, all transformations are tried, and the transformation that results in the greatest overall improvement is chosen. That transformation is added to the ordered list of transformations and applied to the text, and then the next iteration is performed.

Using `tgrep`, a corpus grep utility, Brill & Resnik extracted 4-tuples of the form "Verb $Noun_1$ Preposition $Noun_2$" from the parsed WSJ corpus; this resulted in 12,800 cases. The data was split into 12,300 training cases, and 500 evaluation cases. The method learned transformations of the following form:

```
Change attachment from (N,V) to (V, N) if:

Noun₁ is wordᵢ
Noun₂ is wordⱼ
Verb is wordₖ
Preposition is wordₗ
Noun₁ is wordᵢ and Noun₂ is wordⱼ
Noun₁ is wordᵢ and Verb is wordⱼ
...
```

Rules were allowed to match any combination of up to three words. The initial accuracy (Right Association) was 64%. At the end, after 471 transformations were learned, average accuracy was 80.8%. In a second experiment, the matching was generalized to use synonym classes from WORDNET. After learning only 266 rules, the overall accuracy increased to 81.8%.

2.6 Critique of Previous Approaches

This section summarizes the main advantages and problems with the previous approaches to ambiguity resolution that have been described in this chapter.

2.6.1 Syntactic Approaches

Syntactic factors clearly play a large role in ambiguity resolution. For example, it seems that over 50% of cases of structural ambiguity is resolved in accordance with the principle of Right Association.

At the same time, the syntactic principles for disambiguation, such as "Minimal Attachment" and "Right Association, suffer from a variety of problems. First of all, the effect of these two principles depends on the exact rules that are assumed in the grammar. For example, as first noted by by [Church, 1980], the predictions made by these principles regarding PP attachment depend entirely on which phrase structure rules are assumed. Assuming that Minimal Attachment is decisive, the following set of rules would predict attachment to the verb phrase:

VP $\longrightarrow$ V NP PP*
NP $\longrightarrow$ NP PP
NP $\longrightarrow$ Det Noun

The prediction can be reversed, however, by instead assuming the following set of rules:

VP $\longrightarrow$ VP PP
NP $\longrightarrow$ Det Noun PP*

Even if this basic flaw is disregarded and a particular set of grammar rules is chosen, the principles still fail to make the proper predictions for many cases. For example, [Gibson, 1991] lists a number of problematic sentences. For example, consider this minimal pair where PP attachment differs due to semantic and pragmatic reasons:

a. Mary read the article in the bathtub.   (2.11)
b. Mary read the article in the magazine.

Furthermore, it is widely acknowledged that many cases of structural ambiguity, including PP attachment ambiguity, cannot be resolved on the basis of structural properties of the sentence alone. Semantic or pragmatic information is also required. See, for example, [Taraban et al., 1990]. To illustrate this points, consider the following sentence where the proper attachment can not be determined without further context:

I want that car in the picture.   (2.12)

2.6.2 Semantic and Pragmatic Approaches

Semantic and pragmatic principles account for additional factors that are ignored by purely syntactic approaches. However, these approaches also suffer from a variety of shortcomings.

As demonstrated by [Gibson, 1991], the specific principle of lexical preference proposed by Ford, Bresnan, and Kaplan, as well as the specific pragmatic principles of Crain and Steedman, make wrong predictions in many cases. Gibson concludes that while both studies were successful in pointing out necessary *components* of ambiguity resolution, these principles in isolation do not constitute an empirically adequate theory.

The models based on the AI approach of commonsense semantics suffer from different sorts of problems. As [Jacobs et al., 1991] observes, this approach works best for small, well-defined domains; attacking a larger domain would require a huge, well-orchestrated knowledge engineering effort. These types of systems are difficult to program and debug. Many of the earlier parsing systems based on the commonsense semantics approach missed significant syntactic generalizations. This makes it difficult to achieve broad grammatical coverage, and to port the system to a new domain. Manual rule acquisition for these models is a very expensive process.

The pragmatic principles described by Crain & Steedman presuppose a rather extensive infrastructure that includes world and domain knowledge, a dynamic discourse model, presupposition and entailment computation, etc., which goes quite far beyond the current state of the art.

2.6.3 Corpus-based Approaches

Corpus-based approaches to ambiguity resolution have focused attention on lexical preferences, and have provided some elementary tools for training probabilistic models from natural language data.

At the same time, previous work on corpus-based approaches to modeling ambiguity resolution has stopped short of constructing sound statistical models of the phenomena under study. Often, the approach is limited to obtaining probabilities directly from the observed frequencies. For example, the approach to handling unknown words described in [Magerman and Marcus, 1991] is to assume the distribution over open class lexical categories that was observed in the training corpus.

In some other cases, attention is limited to only one statistical variable, even though there are other features that are likely to have an impact on the phenomenon under question. For example, the approach to PP attachment disambiguation described by [Hindle and Rooth, 1993] is restricted to estimating the "lexical association" between prepositions and attachment sites, which is based on observed co-occurrence between verbs/nouns and prepositions.

Some studies that have used more than one feature were marred by ad-hoc independence assumptions, which were neither motivated by intuitive arguments, nor supported by statistical tests showing that there is little correlation between different features. For example, the model for unknown words described by [Weischedel et al., 1993] is based on four features, but the probability distributions for the features are estimated independently, and are combined as if they were independent, by simple multiplication of the terms arising from each feature. The same oversimplification exists in stochastic Part-of-Speech tagging, which is based on considerable independence assumptions; see Section 5.1.2 for further details. In the next chapter, we will see how our approach rises above all of these limitations.

3. Loglinear Models for Ambiguity Resolution

This section describes the loglinear approach to the problem of ambiguity resolution. The next section highlights the advantages of this approach, and the remainder of this chapter describes the details of the loglinear method, and presents an example.

3.1 Requirements for Effective Ambiguity Resolution

The previous chapter discussed the main problems of previous approaches to ambiguity resolution. The current approach was designed in response to these shortcomings. There are four main requirements for an effective ambiguity resolution procedure:

3.1.1 Automatic Training

The first concern is to avoid the knowledge acquisition bottleneck that arises from the manual creation of the extensive knowledge sources that are required for traditional methods for disambiguation. The loglinear approach is based on statistical models whose parameters are estimated automatically via an iterative procedure from text corpora. Manual expertise is still required to identify potentially useful features, but the main burden of knowledge acquisition has been removed.

3.1.2 Handling Multiple Features

In order to achieve effective ambiguity resolution, it is necessary to combine multiple disambiguating features. The loglinear method goes beyond the one-dimensional probabilistic models that are currently common in corpus-based computational linguistics, since it provides a way to combine multiple categorical features while taking into account their interactions in a proper Bayesian manner.

3.1.3 Modeling Feature Dependencies

It is not enough to model the "main effects" of a number of features in isolation. Natural language is a complicated and ill-understood phenomenon, and it seems certain that many aspects of language are not independent. For this reason, it is important to choose a modeling technique that allows interactions to be modeled explicitly. Loglinear models were chosen because they allow feature interactions to be modeled directly, by adding *interaction terms* to the model specification.

3.1.4 Robustness

An effective ambiguity resolution procedure must be robust in two senses. First, it must not be limited to a specific domain for which it has been constructed and tuned, most likely at significant expense. Instead, it should have wide applicability, and its performance should degrade gracefully when it is applied to data that has not been covered well during training. Second, the procedure should not be a monolithic black box; it should lend itself to integration with other components that might compensate for some of its inadequacies.

The loglinear method meets both of these requirements. As described in detail in Section 3.3, the loglinear model is based on marginal distributions which represent dimensions along which generalization in the model takes place. Furthermore, the loglinear method delivers a posterior probability distribution over the response variable. This can be integrated with other components of a language analysis device, using, for example, Bayesian updating [Pearl, 1988].

3.2 Ambiguity Resolution as a Classification Problem

As described in Chapter 2, an ambiguous natural language expression has more than one possible interpretation. For example, a word might have more than one possible Part-of-Speech (POS), or a Prepositional Phrase might have more than possible attachment site. This section shows how ambiguity resolution can be viewed as a classification problem.

3.2.1 Making Decisions under Uncertainty

Decision theory is concerned with choosing the "best" action from a set of alternatives. The outcomes of the possible actions depend on a future event, about which the decision-maker is uncertain.

After an action is chosen, and one of the possible uncertain events has occurred, a "payoff" is obtained. For each of the possible events, there is a maximum payoff. All other actions incur a conditional opportunity loss; this is the loss on the payoff, given that one of the events occurred. The loss for the actions that lead to the maximum payoff is zero; for all the other actions, the loss is the maximum payoff for the event, minus the payoff for the action taken.

The decision-maker's uncertainty about the event is encoded in a probability distribution over the possible events. This allows the calculation of the *expected loss* for each possible action.

A decision-maker might care only about payoffs; in that case, he would choose the action that minimizes the expected loss. If considerations other than the payoff are important, the decision-maker tries to maximize a subjective *utility function* that depends both on the payoff, and on the other considerations, such as the degree of uncertainty associated with the payoffs.

3.2.2 Statistical Classification

As shown [Duda and Hart, 1973], the framework of decision theory can be applied to classification problems. The uncertain event corresponds to the correct interpretation for the ambiguous natural language expression. Let $I = \{i_1, \ldots, i_n\}$ be the set of possible interpretations for the expressions.

The possible actions correspond to the different possible classifications. Let $C = \{c_1, \ldots, c_k\}$ be the set of possible classifications. The set C contains all members of I as "individual" classifications, but it also contains multiple classifications that can be viewed as "sets" contained in the power set 2^I. The purpose of these set classifications is to allow the classifier to return answers that still contain some uncertainty, such as "one of the nominal tags" for POS tagging or "one of three closely related senses" for word-sense ambiguity resolution.

The loss function λ describes the loss incurred for classifying an expression in a certain way, given its correct interpretation. Let $\lambda(c_{\text{proposed}}|i_{\text{correct}})$ be the loss incurred for classifying the expression as category c_{proposed}, given that the correct interpretation is i_{correct}.

The features used for classification are encoded as a feature vector $\mathbf{v}$. Thus, an instance of $\mathbf{v}$ corresponds to a particular combination of values for all features. For example, if the features are CAPITALIZATION, PREFIX, and SUFFIX, then the word *superfluous* would result in the feature vector ¡*lower-case*, "*super*", "*ous*"¿.

$P(\mathbf{v}|i_x)$ is the conditional probability distribution for $\mathbf{v}$, given the interpretation i_x. This distribution indicates how the feature values are distributed within each category. For example, for the POS "Proper Noun", a higher probability for feature combinations including the value *upper-case* would be expected.

Let $P(i)$ be the prior probability distribution over interpretations, and $P(\mathbf{v})$ the prior distribution for the features. Given this, Bayes rule can be used to derive the conditional probability distribution for the correct interpretation, given the feature vector:

$$P(i|\mathbf{v}) = \frac{P(\mathbf{v}|i)P(i)}{P(\mathbf{v})} \qquad (3.1)$$

3.2.3 Expected Loss and the Zero-One Loss Function

Suppose we are trying to classify an ambiguous expression with features $\mathbf{v}$. For a proposed classification c_{proposed}, the loss incurred by making that classification is $\lambda(c_{\text{proposed}}, i_{\text{correct}})$. Since the conditional probability for the correct interpretation given the feature vector, $P(i_{\text{correct}}|\mathbf{v})$, can be estimated using Bayes rule, the expected loss for the proposed classification c_{proposed}, given the features $\mathbf{v}$, can be calculated:

$$\text{Expected Conditional Loss}(c_{\text{proposed}}|\mathbf{v}) = \qquad (3.2)$$

$$= \sum_{i_x \in I} P(i_x|\mathbf{v})\lambda(c_{\text{proposed}}|i_x)$$

Suppose the nature of the classification problem is such that there is one correct interpretation, and all other interpretations are equally incorrect. For example, in the case of POS tagging, suppose that there is one correct POS tag for each word, and all other tags are equally incorrect.

This is expressed with a "zero-one" loss function. A zero-one loss function assigns zero loss to the correct classification, and a loss of one unit to all other classifications. That is, if the correct interpretation is i_{correct}, then

$$\lambda(c_{\text{proposed}}|i_{\text{correct}}) = \begin{cases} 0 & \text{if } i_{\text{correct}} \in c_{\text{proposed}} \\ 1 & \text{otherwise} \end{cases} \qquad (3.3)$$

3.2.4 Minimum Error Rate Classification

If a zero-one loss function is used, the loss for the correct classification is 0, and the expected conditional loss for a proposed classification c_{proposed} is as follows:

$$\text{Expected Conditional Loss}(c_{\text{proposed}}|\mathbf{v}) \qquad (3.4)$$

$$= \sum_{i_x \in I} P(i_x|\mathbf{v})\lambda(c_{\text{proposed}}|i_x)$$

$$= \sum_{i_x \neq i_{\text{correct}}} P(i_x|\mathbf{v})$$

$$= 1 - P(i_{\text{correct}}$$
$$= c_{\text{proposed}}|\mathbf{v})$$

$P(c_{\text{proposed}}|\mathbf{v})$ is the conditional probability that c_{proposed} is the correct classification. The expected conditional loss is the probability of choosing an incorrect classification. Thus, minimizing expected loss corresponds to minimizing the probability of error. This is called *minimum error rate* classification [Duda and Hart, 1973].

3.2.5 Maximizing Utility

With a zero-one loss function and only individual classifications, minimum-error-rate classification can be performed by maximizing the conditional probability $P(c_{\text{proposed}}|\mathbf{v})$, and choosing the mode of the posterior distribution. A zero-one loss function is not always appropriate, however, and minimizing expected loss is not sufficient when set classifications are allowed.

A zero-one loss function is not appropriate if the set of possible interpretations has some relevant structure. For example, for the problem of word-sense disambiguation, the loss function could return a continuous value that indicates the distance to the correct meaning. As another example, Section 2.5.2 describes some systematic difficulties with deciding correct PP attachment. In some cases, different PP attachments make no semantic difference, and it is impossible for a human judge looking at the full context to decide the correct attachment. In these cases, it does not make sense to consider one interpretation correct, and all other interpretations equally incorrect.

Set classifications can be useful for a number of different purposes. The set of possible interpretations might have some structure. For example, the set of possible senses for a given word might not be a "flat list", but might instead be structured with some senses being very different from each other, while some other senses are closely related. In this case, the closely related senses could be grouped into clusters that correspond to set classifications. Set classifications can also be used if the purpose of the classifier is to reduce uncertainty to some degree, but only as far as possible at that stage, and to carry some remaining ambiguity to be resolved at a later stage when other types of information can be brought to be bear in the problem. In such a case, the classification set could consist of some of the more likely interpretations. For example, the unknown word model described below that supplies lexical probabilities returns a probability distribution over the tags that the word is likely to take on, and the remaining ambiguity is resolved with the aid of contextual probabilities.

If the loss function is not zero-one, or if there are set classifications that do not fit into the scheme of minimum-error-rate classification, a more subtle decision rule is required. A "utility function" can be defined that describes how the usefulness of a proposed classification depends on the expected loss, and on some other relevant characteristics. For natural language ambiguity resolution, one such characteristic is the *residual ambiguity* of the classification set. The residual ambiguity is defined as the perplexity of the individual interpretations in the set (see Section 1.2.1).

In practice, the best utility function depends on the exact nature of the application. The tradeoff between accuracy and residual ambiguity encountered in the unknown word modeling experiments is described in Section 4.3.7 below.

3.3 The Loglinear Model

This section describes the details of constructing a model of ambiguity resolution using a loglinear model.

3.3.1 Categorical Data Analysis

A feature or characteristic of the objects in a domain under investigation whose value is collected, summarized, and analyzed is called a statistical variable. The value of a *categorical* statistical variable consists of one of a set of categories. For example, the variable POLITICAL-PERSUASION might have values such as *conservative, liberal, socialist,* etc. An example of a linguistic variable is PART-OF-SPEECH; its possible values include *noun, verb, determiner, preposition,* etc.[1]

3.3.2 The Contingency Table

We distinguish between a set of *explanatory* variables, and one *response* variable. The statistical model is used to perform the following inference: Given the values of the explanatory variables, what is the value of the response variable? Or, more precisely, given the values of the explanatory variables, what is the probability distribution for the response variable, i.e., what are the probabilities for the different possible values of the response variable?

The basic tool used in Categorical Data Analysis is the contingency table, or the "cross-classified table of counts". A contingency table has one dimension for each variable, including the response variable. Each cell in the contingency table records the frequency of data with the appropriate characteristics.

Let's consider a simple example. Suppose the task of the model is to predict the Part-of-Speech of an unknown word, based on whether the word is capitalized, whether it includes a hyphen, and whether it carries one of the English inflectional suffixes. This means there are four categorical variables:

---

[1] In the experiments, the Part-of-Speech (POS) tagset from the Treebank project (shown in Appendix B) is used. The open class tags from this tagset are shown in Table 4.1.

1. **POS**. Possible values: *noun, verb, adjective, adverb*.
2. **CAPITALIZED**. Possible values: *upper-case, lower-case*.
3. **HYPHENATED**. Possible values: *hyphen, no-hyphen*.
4. **INFLECTION**. Possible values: *er, est, ed, ing, s, ly, no-inflection*.

Some training data are gathered. Then, the contingency table is constructed, and each word in the training sample is cross-classified according to its features.

The contingency table has four dimensions: **POS, CAPITALIZED, HYPHENATED**, and **INFLECTION**. Each dimension has the appropriate number of values, so the entire table has $4 * 2 * 2 * 7 = 112$ cells. Each cell holds the count for the number of times that a word with the appropriate features has been observed in the training data. For example, using the feature values as array indices, the cell ¡*verb, lower-case, no-hyphen, ing*¿ will hold the number of lower-case verbs without a hyphen that carry the *-ing* suffix.

Each cell concerns a specific combination of features. This provides a way to estimate probabilities of specific feature combinations from the observed frequencies, as the cell counts can easily be converted to probabilities. Classification is achieved by determining the value of the response variable (**POS**) given the values of the explanatory variables (**CAPITALIZATION, HYPHENATION, INFLECTION.**) The probabilities can be used directly for Bayesian statistical inference, obtaining a probability distribution that is properly conditioned on the combinations of the values of the explanatory variables. Thus, it is not necessary to make any independence assumptions between the features. Section 3.4 explains this in more detail.

3.3.3 The Importance of Smoothing

One of the main problems in statistical modeling, including corpus-based computational linguistics, is the problem of sparse data. Statistical samples from text corpora are usually *effectively small* [Good, 1965]. That is, parameter estimates based directly on observed frequencies would reflect idiosyncrasies of the training data, and not provide a good estimate of the population under study. One particular problem concerns "sampling zeros", events that are not present in the training data. Direct estimation would assign all these events a probability of 0, even though it is very likely indeed that the probability of some of these events is bigger than 0. For this reason, estimated probabilities are usually *smoothed* to remove idiosyncrasies of the sample, and to provide a better estimation of the probabilities of events in the domain under investigation.

A loglinear model can be employed as a "smoothing device, used to obtain cell estimates for every cell in a sparse array, even if the observed count is zero"[Bishop et al., 1975]. A loglinear model is a model of the effect of the explanatory variables and their combinations on the response variable. The observed counts from the training data are used to estimate the parameters for the model; the model then provides estimated expected counts. These counts are smoother than the training data; they reflect less of the idiosyncrasies of the training data sample.

3.3.4 Individual Cells

The model is called "loglinear" because its mathematical form is a linear combination of the logs of cell counts. Let us introduce some terminology and notation that is used with loglinear models. The possible   values of a variable are called "levels". The number of levels is usually denoted by one of the letters I, J, K, etc. N denotes the sample size. So, in the above example, the first variable is POS, and I=4. Observed cell counts are denoted by a lower-case x with the appropriate subscript. For example, $x_{1,1,1,1}$ is the cell count at the fist level of the first variable, the first level of the second variable, and so on. More generally, x_{ijkl} is the observed cell count at level i of the first variable, level j of the second variable, and so on.

The cell counts can be viewed as random variables. The expected values of the cell counts are denoted by a lower-case m with the appropriate subscripts. Thus, $m_{1,1,1,1}$ is the expected cell count for cell (1,1,1,1). The purpose of the loglinear model is to estimate these expected values. In order to distinguish between the expected cell count, and the estimates of the expected cell counts produced by the model, the estimated expected cell counts are denoted by the symbol $\hat{m}_{ijkl}$. The probabilities derived from cell frequencies are denoted by $\hat{p}_{ijkl}$.

3.3.5 Marginal Totals and Expected Cell Counts

Given a contingency table, the cell entries can be summed up in various ways. Such sums are called *marginal totals*. For example, all cell counts where the first variable is at level 1 can be summed up. This sum is denoted by x_{1+++}:

$$x_{1+++} = \sum_{j=1}^{J} \sum_{k=1}^{K} \sum_{l=1}^{L} x_{1jkl} \tag{3.5}$$

In general, a marginal total is denoted by replacing the subscripts for the dimensions that are summed over by a plus sign. So, the total for the ith level of the first variable is denoted by x_{i+++}; the total for the ith level of the first variable and the jth level of the second variable is denoted by x_{ij++}; the ith level for the first variable, jth level for the second variable, and kth level for the third variable is x_{ijk+}. x_{++++} stands for the total for the entire table.

Suppose all the variables in the example were independent. Then, the expected cell counts would be the product of the individual probabilities of the levels of each variable, known as the *main effects*. The main effects are estimated from the marginal totals x_{i+++}, x_{+j++}, x_{++k+}, and x_{+++l}. x_{i+++}, for example, corresponds to the effect of the first variable being at level i. (To understand what this means, recall that $\frac{x_{i+++}}{N}$ is the fraction of all samples with the first variable at level i.) Assuming independence between the variables, the expected cell counts are given by the following formula:

$$m_{ijkl} = \frac{x_{i+++}x_{+j++}x_{++k+}x_{+++l}}{N^3} \tag{3.6}$$

This is the model for complete independence of the variables. Contrary to the assumptions made implicitly or explicitly by previous work in corpus-based language modeling (see Section 2), complete independence between variables usually doesn't hold in natural language modeling. A loglinear model provides a way to estimate expected cell counts that depend not only on the main effects of the variables, but also on the interactions between variables.

The derivation proceeds as follows. Taking the logarithm of Equation 3.6 yields the following expression:

$$\log m_{ijkl} = \tag{3.7}$$
$$= \log x_{i+++} + \log x_{+j++} + \log x_{++k+} + \log x_{+++l} - 3logN$$

Equation 3.7 has an additive form that suggests expressing the parameter m_{ijkl} as a sum of effect terms [Fienberg, 1980]:

$$\log m_{ijkl} = u + u_{1(i)} + u_{2(j)} + u_{3(k)} + u_{4(l)} \tag{3.8}$$

In Equation 3.8, u is the mean of the logarithms of all the expected counts, $u + u_{1(i)}$ is the mean of the logarithms of the expected counts at level i of the first variable, $u + u_{2(j)}$ is the mean of the logarithms of the expected counts at level j of the second variable, and so on. This can be illustrated with the following example:

$$u + u_{1(i)} = \frac{1}{JKL} \sum_{j=1}^{J} \sum_{k=1}^{K} \sum_{l=1}^{L} \log m_{ijkl} \tag{3.9}$$

The term $u_{1(i)}$ represents the deviation of the expected cell counts at level i of the first variable from the grand mean u.

3.3.6 Interdependent Variables and Interaction Terms

So far, only the model of independence has been considered. Dependence between variables is introduced into the model by adding *interaction terms*. Interaction terms represent the combined effect of the levels of more than variable. For example, the term $u_{12(ij)}$ represents the effect of the ith level of the first variable *and* the jth level of the second variable.

The notion of interaction term is central to loglinear models. Given a problem with a set of variables, a loglinear model is specified by the interaction terms that are included. A convenient shorthand for specifying models consists of listing the variables of the interaction terms that are included in the following manner:

[1] [2] [3]

This specifies three interaction terms, each concerning only one variable — the model for complete independence of the variables. Only a subset of loglinear models called *hierarchical models* will be considered. A model is hierarchical if, for each higher-order interaction term, the related lower-order terms are included. For example, if a hierarchical loglinear model includes the interaction term [123] $(u_{123(ijk)})$, then it also includes the terms [1], [2], [3], [12], [13], and [23]. These lower-order terms are usually omitted from the model specifications.

As an example, recall the earlier example with four variables. Some of the possible loglinear models for this problem are shown in Table 3.1.

Table 3.1. Some Loglinear Model Specifications

Specification	Explanation
[1] [2] [3] [4]	Model for independence
[12] [3] [4]	Variables 1 and 2 interact
[12] [13] [14] [23] [24] [34]	All second-order interactions included, but no higher-order interactions.
[1234]	All interaction terms included (saturated model)

3.3.7 The Iterative Estimation Procedure

The goal of model estimation is to calculate the estimated expected cell counts, given the model specification. In general, the expected cell counts are given by a formula of the following form:

$$\log m_{ijk...} = u + u_{1(i)} + u_{2(j)} + u_{3(k)} + u_{12(ij)} + \cdots \qquad (3.10)$$

For some simple models, it is possible to obtain closed forms for the expected cell counts. (A "closed form" is an algebraic expression that allows the value to be computed in one step.) For more complicated models, an iterative estimation procedure is used. The *iterative proportional fitting* algorithm for hierarchical loglinear models was first presented by [Deming and Stephan, 1940]. This procedure is explained below.

The interaction terms in the loglinear models represent constraints on the estimated expected marginal totals. Each of these marginal constraints translates into an adjustment scaling factor for the cell entries. The iterative procedure has the following steps:

1. Start with initial estimates for the estimated expected cell counts. For example, set all $\hat{m}_{ijkl} = 1.0$.
2. Adjust each cell entry by multiplying it with the scaling factors. This moves the cell entries towards satisfaction of the marginal constraints.
3. Iterate through the adjustment steps until the maximum difference ϵ between the marginal totals observed in the sample and the estimated marginal totals reaches a preset minimum threshold, e.g. $\epsilon = 0.1$.

After each cycle, the estimates satisfy the constraints specified in the model, and the estimated expected marginal totals come closer to matching the observed totals. Thus, the process converges. This results in Maximum Likelihood estimates for both multinomial and   independent Poisson sampling schemes [Agresti, 1990].

3.3.8 Example of Iterative Estimation

An example illustrates this procedure. Consider the following model:

[12] [13] [14] [23] [24] [34]

This model has the following mathematical form:

$$\log m_{ijkl} = \qquad\qquad (3.11)$$
$$= u + u_{1(i)} + u_{2(j)} + u_{3(k)} + u_{4(l)} + u_{12(ij)} + u_{13(ik)} +$$
$$+ u_{14(il)} + u_{23(jk)} + u_{24(jl)} + u_{34(kl)}$$

This model leads to the following marginal constraints:

$$
\begin{array}{rcll}
\hat{m}_{++++} &=& x_{++++} & (u) \\
\hat{m}_{i+++} &=& x_{i+++} & (u_1) \\
\hat{m}_{+j++} &=& x_{+j++} & (u_2) \\
\hat{m}_{++k+} &=& x_{++k+} & (u_3) \\
\hat{m}_{+++l} &=& x_{+++l} & (u_4) \\
\hat{m}_{ij++} &=& x_{ij++} & (u_{12}) \\
\hat{m}_{i+k+} &=& x_{i+k+} & (u_{13}) \\
\hat{m}_{i++l} &=& x_{i++l} & (u_{14}) \\
\hat{m}_{+jk+} &=& x_{+jk+} & (u_{23}) \\
\hat{m}_{+j+l} &=& x_{+j+l} & (u_{24}) \\
\hat{m}_{++kl} &=& x_{++kl} & (u_{34})
\end{array}
$$

(3.12)

Because some of the constraints subsume some others, only the following constraints need to be considered:

$$\begin{aligned}
\hat{m}_{ij++} &= x_{ij++} \\
\hat{m}_{i+k+} &= x_{i+k+} \\
\hat{m}_{i++l} &= x_{i++l} \\
\hat{m}_{+jk+} &= x_{+jk+} \\
\hat{m}_{+j+l} &= x_{+j+l} \\
\hat{m}_{++kl} &= x_{++kl}
\end{aligned} \tag{3.13}$$

Each of these marginal constraints defines one adjustment scaling factor. For example, the constraint $\hat{m}_{ij++} = x_{ij++}$ translates into the following adjustment scaling factor, where n and $n+1$ refer to successive iterations:

$$\hat{m}_{ijkl}^{n+1} = \frac{x_{ij++}}{\hat{m}_{ij++}^{n}} \hat{m}_{ijkl}^{n} \tag{3.14}$$

Since this is an iterative procedure, update steps are counted with a superscript: Let $\hat{m}_{ijkl}^{n}$ be the estimated expected cell count after the nth update steps. For this example, there are six update steps per iteration of the estimation procedure. Iterations are counted with the variable t: $\hat{m}_{ijkl}^{6t+1}$ is the value after the first update step in the tth iteration. The steps below are carried out for $t = 0, 1, 2, \ldots$ until the estimated and observed marginal totals converge so that the maximal difference is less than the preset threshold ϵ.

1. Set $\hat{m}_{ijkl}^{6t+1} = \frac{x_{ij++}}{\hat{m}_{ij++}^{6t}} \hat{m}_{ijkl}^{6t}$ for all i, j, k, l

2. Set $\hat{m}_{ijkl}^{6t+2} = \frac{x_{i+k+}}{\hat{m}_{i+k+}^{6t+1}} \hat{m}_{ijkl}^{6t+1}$ for all i, j, k, l

3. Set $\hat{m}_{ijkl}^{6t+3} = \frac{x_{i++l}}{\hat{m}_{i++l}^{6t+2}} \hat{m}_{ijkl}^{6t+2}$ for all i, j, k, l

4. Set $\hat{m}_{ijkl}^{6t+4} = \frac{x_{+jk+}}{\hat{m}_{+jk+}^{6t+3}} \hat{m}_{ijkl}^{6t+3}$ for all i, j, k, l

5. Set $\hat{m}_{ijkl}^{6t+5} = \frac{x_{+j+l}}{\hat{m}_{+j+l}^{6t+4}} \hat{m}_{ijkl}^{6t+4}$ for all i, j, k, l

6. Set $\hat{m}_{ijkl}^{6t+6} = \frac{x_{++kl}}{\hat{m}_{++kl}^{6t+5}} \hat{m}_{ijkl}^{6t+5}$ for all i, j, k, l

The result of this fitting procedure is a contingency table with smoothed counts. This table is then used to perform the inference.

3.3.9 Definition of a Loglinear Model

The general form of a loglinear model was shown in Equation 3.10. For the purpose of the current work, a specific instance of a loglinear model can be defined to consist of the following:

- A set of categorical variables $X, Y, Z, \ldots$ One of the variables is designated as the response variable.
- For each variable, a set of levels (possible values). For example, variable X might have I levels $x_1, x_2, \ldots, x_I$.
- A set of interaction terms that specifies the exact form of the expression relating expected cell counts with marginal totals. For example, [12] [23] specifies the model where variables X and Y are independent, given Z.

— A termination threshold ϵ that determines when to stop the iterative estimation procedure.

3.4 Statistical Inference

Let us summarize the modeling procedure. A set of explanatory variables E, and a response variable R, are determined. A training sample is obtained, and it is cross-classified according to all the variables. Next, the contingency table is constructed. The table is smoothed using a loglinear model, resulting in a table with estimated expected counts. Then, the table is used to obtain a conditional probability distribution over the response variable R, given values for the explanatory variables E. This section shows how this can be viewed as an application of Bayes rule. The conditional distribution is available directly from the table, so the derivation shown in this section is for expository purposes only, and not a sequence of calculations that is actually performed when the model is applied.

3.4.1 The Bayesian Approach

In the words of [Good, 1965], "the essential defining property of a Bayesian is that he regards it as meaningful to talk about the probability $P(H|E)$ of a hypothesis H, given evidence E." Bayes rule tells us how the conditional probability $P(H|E)$ can be expressed in terms of the probabilities $P(H)$ and $P(E)$, and the conditional probability $P(E|H)$.

This applies to the current approach in the following way. The goal is to obtain a probability distribution for the response variable, R. The "evidence" comes in the shape of observations of the word features, which assign values to the explanatory variables E:

$$P(R|E) = \frac{P(E|R)P(R)}{P(E)} \tag{3.15}$$

The smoothed contingency table provides estimates for the quantities on the right-hand side of this equation. $P(R)$ corresponds to the marginal totals summing over all variables, except for the response variable R. $P(E)$ corresponds to the marginal totals summed over the response variable. $P(E|R)$ corresponds to the individual cell entries.

3.4.2 Bayesian Inference using the Contingency Table

Recall the earlier example for guessing the POS of an unknown word. The first variable, POS, is the response variable, and the remaining three variables are explanatory variables. The model is used to infer the probability function for POS given values for the explanatory variables. Let $p(R = r_i)$ be the prior probability of the response variable having level i. Let $p(E = e_{jkl})$ be the probability of the explanatory variables having levels j, k, l. Then,

$$p(R = r_i) \quad = \quad \frac{\hat{m}_{i+++}}{\hat{m}_{++++}} \tag{3.16}$$

$$p(E = e_{jkl}) \quad = \quad \frac{\hat{m}_{+jkl}}{\hat{m}_{++++}} \tag{3.17}$$

$$p(E = e_{jkl}|R = r_i) \quad = \quad \frac{\hat{m}_{ijkl}}{\hat{m}_{i+++}} \tag{3.18}$$

Substitution into Bayes rule (Equation 3.15) yields the following:

$$P(R = r_i|E = e_{jkl}) \quad = \quad \frac{P(E = e_{jkl}|R = r_i)P(R = r_i)}{P(E = e_{jkl})} \tag{3.19}$$

$$= \quad \frac{\frac{\hat{m}_{ijkl}}{\hat{m}_{i+++}}\frac{\hat{m}_{i+++}}{\hat{m}_{++++}}}{\frac{\hat{m}_{+jkl}}{\hat{m}_{++++}}}$$

$$= \quad \frac{\frac{\hat{m}_{ijkl}}{\hat{m}_{++++}}}{\frac{\hat{m}_{+jkl}}{\hat{m}_{++++}}}$$

$$= \quad \frac{\hat{m}_{ijkl}}{\hat{m}_{+jkl}}$$

In summary, the probabilities $P(R)$ and $P(E)$ correspond to the marginal totals $\hat{m}_{i+++}$ and $\hat{m}_{+jkl}$, and the posterior probability $P(R|E)$ can be calculated directly from the cell entry $\hat{m}_{ijkl}$ and the marginal total $\hat{m}_{+jkl}$.

3.5 Exploratory Data Analysis

The preceding sections have described the formal aspects of the loglinear modeling technique. There is another aspect, however, which has to do with selecting the variables, table shapes, and interaction terms for the smoothing model.

A set of data does not come with instructions for its analysis. Which aspects of the data should be modeled? Which variables should be chosen? What should be chosen as the levels (possible values) for the variables? For the loglinear model, which variables are in dependent, and which variables interact?

3.5.1 The Exploratory Nature of this Approach

In practice, there are no exact methods for answering these questions. Instead, one must search for answers to these questions by exploring the data to look for variables that are good discriminators, trying out different combinations of variables, performing experiments with different configurations, and comparing the results. This aspect of the art of probabilistic modeling should not be undervalued; indeed, once the approach to the problem has been determined, most time is spent exploring different configurations, feature sets and smoothing models.

3.5.2 Searching for Discriminators

How is the exploratory analysis performed? First, the problem is analyzed, and possibly relevant features of the data are determined. Possible values for the features are considered, and their effects on the data are examined. In order to maintain the integrity of the experimental setup, a strict division is maintained between the training sample and possibly other sets of data that may be examined, and a different set of evaluation data that must not be examined or used in any way.

The data is explored to determine how well different feature/value combinations serve to discriminate in the response variable. Some of this exploration can be based on graphs that indicate the discriminatory power of different features, Experiments with different interaction terms for the loglinear model are also performed, in order to determine an appropriate set of interaction terms.

It is difficult to predict how well a given combination of features, levels, and smoothing terms will actually perform. For this reason, a large part of the exploration consists of evaluating different models on evaluation data, and measuring the performance of the different configurations. Based on insights from the exploration, variables can be added or deleted, and the number of levels for the variables can be changed. This has the effect of changing the shape of the contingency table. By deleting features or some levels of features, parts of the table are merged, and the table is "coarsened". By adding features or introducing finer distinctions in the levels of a variable, more cells are introduced, and the table is "refined". Also, different interactions between the variables can be specified in the loglinear model.

4. Modeling New Words

The first series of experiments concerns the problem of new or *unknown* words. No computational lexicon can be complete; new words are coined frequently, and established words are used in novel ways. Thus, any natural language analysis system must be prepared to deal with words that have never been encountered before.

This chapter only deals with modeling unknown words in isolation. Of course, context, such as the Parts-of-Speech (POSs) of the surrounding words, also provides powerful clues. Stochastic POS taggers require a lexicon that includes probabilities of words taking on specific POSs. A full POS tagger integrates the evidence provided by context with the lexical probabilities provided by the lexicon and the unknown word model; this is described in Chapter 5.

4.1 Experimental Data and Procedure

First, let us describe the data that was used in the experiments, and the procedure that was followed.

4.1.1 Problem Statement

A robust syntactic analysis procedure must include a component that can predict the likely POSs of an unknown word, based on characteristics of the word. This component is called the unknown word model. The unknown word model accepts a word about which there is no information in the computational lexicon, and returns a probability distribution over all open class POS tags.

4.1.2 Experimental Data

The experiments use the tagged and bracketed texts from the Treebank project. This includes the following texts:

- **Tagged Brown Corpus.** The Brown Corpus, as retagged by the Tree-bank. This consists of 1.15 million words of text taken from different sources so as to provide samples of different genres of written American English. The corpus is arranged in 500 files of ca. 2,000 words each.

- **Tagged Wall Street Journal Corpus.** 2.64 million words of Wall Street Journal articles. This consists of 6,000 files of varying length.
- **Bracketed Brown Corpus.** The entire Brown Corpus, bracketed by the Penn Treebank project.
- **Bracketed Wall Street Journal Texts.** 880,000 words (35,000 sentences) of Wall Street Journal articles. There are 2,000 files of varying length.

The Penn Treebank reports an error rate for the tagged texts of 2–3%. The parsed texts also include some mistakes. The tagset (the set of POS categories) used by the Penn Treebank is the result of a "radical reduction of the tagset" after a general trend towards bigger and bigger tagsets. There are 48 POS tags in total. Of these, 21 tags are for open class categories, 15 are for closed class categories, and 12 deal with punctuation. The entire tagset for the Treebank is listed in Appendix B; Table 4.1 lists the open class tags.

Table 4.1. Open Class Wordtags Used in the Penn Treebank

Tag	Part of Speech	Example
CD	Cardinal (number)	500,000
FW	Foreign word	Fahrvergnügen
JJ	Adjective	yellow, large
JJR	Comparative Adjective	larger, nicer
JJS	Superlative adjective	largest, nicest
LS	List item marker	1. ..., a) ...
NN	Singular or mass noun	water, rock
NNS	Plural noun	rocks, cars
NNP	Singular proper noun	English, March
NNPS	Plural proper noun	The *English*
RB	Adverb	quickly, quite
RBR	Comparative Adverb	wiser, deeper
RBS	Superlative adverb	nearest, best
SYM	Symbol	%, *
UH	Interjection	uh, hmpf
VB	Base form verb	do, go
VBD	Past tense verb	did, went
VBG	Present participle verb	doing, going
VBN	Past participle verb	gone, flown
VBP	Non-3sg present verb	do, go
VBZ	3sg present verb	does, goes

4.1.3 Modeling Procedure

To obtain training and evaluation samples, the Brown corpus was divided at random into three sets. The division was performed on a file-by-file basis, so that repetitions of words within files were confined to individual sets, and a better model of new text would be obtained.

1. A set S_1 containing 400,000 words was selected to represent the "known words."
2. A set S_2 containing 300,000 words was selected to represent the new text. Every word in S_2 but not in S_1 is considered an unknown word. These unknown words make up the training sample.
3. A third set S_3 containing 300,000 words was selected to evaluate the model. Every word in S_3 but not in S_2 was used as an unknown word for evaluation.

For the final evaluation, there were 17,302 training words, and 21,375 evaluation words. The modeling procedure is as follows:

1. A set of features and possible values for the features is determined.
2. Each word/tag combination in the training sample is classified according to a set of features. This results in a feature vector for each training token.
3. The feature vectors are turned into a contingency table. (See Appendix F for details concerning input to and output from the unknown word model.)
4. The contingency table is smoothed using a loglinear model.
5. The smoothed contingency table is used to classify each unknown word in the evaluation data. Performance figures for accuracy, residual ambiguity, and number of tags in cutoff-factor answer sets are kept.
6. The performance figures are summarized and analyzed.

The actual modeling process is highly experimental, and these steps are carried out for a number of iterations.

4.2 Exploring the Data

This section describes the process of experimenting with different feature sets, feature values, and smoothing terms.

4.2.1 The Initial Feature Set

The first step is to examine a portion of the training data, and to determine an initial set of features. The initial list for the unknown word model is shown below.

- INCLUDES-NUMBER. Does the word include a number? Positive example: *836-901*. Negative example: *Absent-minded*.
- CAPITALIZED. Is the first character of the word a capitalized letter? Positive example: *Abnormal*. Negative examples: *catch, 500,000*.
- INCLUDES-PERIOD. Does the word include a period? Positive examples: *B.C., 4.2, U.N.* Negative example: *Union*.
- INCLUDES-COMMA. Does the word include a comma? Positive example: *500,000*. Negative example: *amazement*.
- FINAL-PERIOD. Is the last character of the word a period? Positive examples: *B.C., Co.* Negative examples: *U.N, Command*.
- INCLUDES-HYPHEN. Does the word include a hyphen? Positive examples: *Poynting-Robertson, anti-party*. Negative example: *answer*.
- SENTENCE-INITIAL. Is the word the first word in the sentence? This feature comes from the context of the word, and its value is determined by looking at the original Treebank file.
- ALL-UPPER-CASE. Is the word in all upper case? "All upper case" is defined as the absence of any lower case letters. Thus, words without any letters at all are also in "all upper case". Positive examples: *CTCA, 1532*. Negative examples: *Fred, accomplish*.
- SHORT. Is the length of the word three characters or less? Positive examples: *W., Yes, bar, Eta*. Negative examples: *Heaven, 100,000*.
- PREFIX. Does the word carry one of a list of known prefixes? (See Section 4.3.3 for the list of prefixes.)
- SUFFIX. Does the word carry one of a list of known suffixes? (See Section 4.3.3 for the list of suffixes.)

The lists of prefixes and suffixes were derived as follows: First, lists of possible prefixes and suffixes were constructed from [Church, 1986], and from ENGLEX, a morphological parsing lexicon for English.[1] The initial affix lists contained 128 prefixes and 207 suffixes. The lists were subsequently shortened in various ways. Initially, all affixes that actually occurred during training were used. This resulted in 100 prefixes and 189 suffixes. At a later stage, only those affixes that occurred 10 times or more during training were used. This resulted in 86 prefixes and 145 affixes. Subsequently, only those affixes that occurred 200 times or more were used; this final reduction resulted in 26 prefixes and 37 suffixes.

4.2.2 Decreasing the Size of the Model

The initial set of features, prefixes, and suffixes would have lead to an impossibly large contingency table. There are both theoretical and practical reasons why the table size has to be kept small. If the table had many more cells than there are training instances, the smoothing technique would break

---

[1] ENGLEX was created by Evan Antworth of the Summer Institute of Linguistics.

Table 4.2. Inflectional Suffixes Provide POS Hints

POS Tag	Meaning	Inflectional Suffix
JJR	Comparative Adjective	*-er*
JJS	Superlative Adjective	*-est*
RB	Adverb	*-ly*
RBR	Comparative Adverb	*-er*
RBS	Superlative Adverb	*-est*
VBD	Past Form Verb	*-ed*
VBG	Present Participle Form Verb	*-ing*
VBN	Past Participle Form Verb	*-ed*
VBZ	Third Person Singular Form Verb	*-s*

down, and many cell counts would remain zero even after smoothing. Furthermore, there are inherent limitations in the available software and hardware, although advances in memory size and execution speed are rapidly expanding the limits on statistical computations.

Thus, out of necessity, the model was split into two contingency tables. One table handles the affixes, and the other table handles the general word features. This introduces an independence assumption between the affixes and the other features. As shown in Table 4.2, inflectional suffixes provide powerful clues for some open class POSs. In order to compensate for the independence assumption caused by the division into two tables, an INFLECTION feature was added to the second table:

– INFLECTION. Does the word carry one of the following inflectional suffixes? Possible values for this feature: *-ed, -er, -est, -ing, -ly, -s*.

4.2.3 Eliminating Low-Information Features

Next, it was necessary to reduce the dimensionality of the data. There are two ways to achieve this: Reducing the number of features, and reducing the number of possible values for a feature. The number of features can be reduced by merging multiple features into a single feature, and by discarding features that are not good discriminators for the response variable.

The original set of features includes one feature for SENTENCE-INITIAL, and one feature for CAPITALIZED. The intuition behind these two features was to pick out words, like proper nouns, that are capitalized, while compensating for the fact that all sentence-initial words are capitalized. To reduce the number of cells in the contingency table, these two features were initially merged into a single CAPITALIZATION feature with two values: "Capitalized in the middle of a sentence", and "other". However, this did not result in very good performance, because proper nouns in sentence-initial position were treated like words in lower case. Therefore, the CAPITALIZATION feature was changed to have three values: "capitalized in sentence initial po-

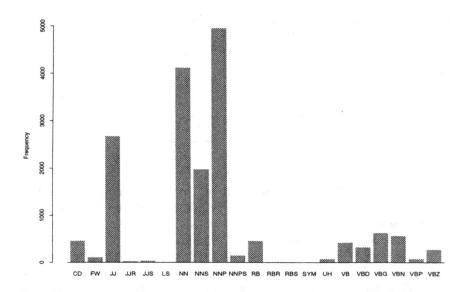

Fig. 4.1. Frequency of Tags in the Training Sample

sition", "capitalized in the middle of the sentence", and "lower case". This reduces the number of cells by a factor of 3/4.

The ability of different features to discriminate between different POSs was also investigated with the aim of excluding features entirely from the model. A plot of the frequency of all tags in the training sample shows the overall distribution of the POS tags. This is shown in Figure 4.1. Next, for each feature, the percentage of tags covered by that feature were plotted. For example, figure 4.2 shows that the NUMBER feature picks out over 95% of the words tagged CD (number), and very few words with other tags.

The percentage plots for the features helped to isolate features of low utility. For example, Figure 4.3 shows the plot for the feature INCLUDES-PERIOD ("one of the characters in the word is a period"). Only 12% of the symbols (SYM) and less than 5% of the interjections (UH) respond to this feature, so it was dropped from the model.

In contrast, Figure 4.4 shows the percentage of tags covered for words that end in an -s. Note how well plural common nouns (NNS), plural proper nouns (NNPS), and third person singular verbs (VBZ) are picked out. At the same time, not insignificant percentages of foreign words (FW), interjections (UH), and singular proper nouns (NNP) are included.

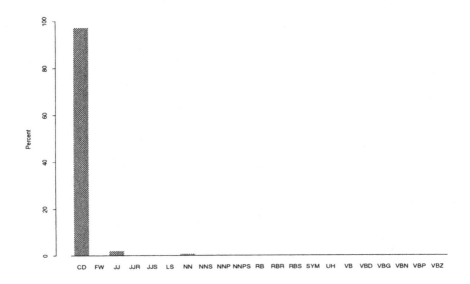

Fig. 4.2. Percentage of Tags for Words that Include a Number

A number of experiments compared the performance of different feature sets. This eventually resulted in the final feature set described in Section 4.3.3 below. In general, a good feature has a number of properties: It discriminates well between different POSs   picking out a large percentage of some POSs, and only a small percentage of the other POSs. Some features subsume other features in their coverage, and in such cases the most general feature should be determined. It is *not* necessary to find features that pick out individual POSs, since one of the central features of the loglinear model is that it is able to handle situations that require the combination of features.

4.2.4 Choosing the Interaction Terms

Finally, the last area for experimentation concerns the interaction terms for the loglinear model. The loglinear model is used to smooth   the cell counts in the contingency table. By measuring the performance of a loglinear model with only the main effects (the model assuming independence between features), it can be verified that the interactions between the features are important.

This can be illustrated with the following example. Taken from a separate set of experiments, Table 4.3 summarizes the performance of different loglinear models while the feature set was being held constant to a set of 5

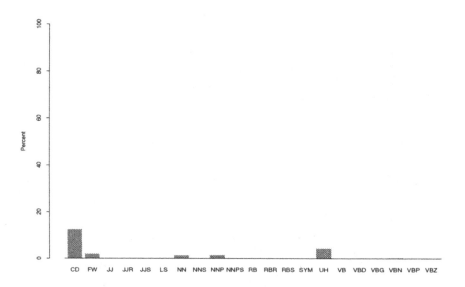

Fig. 4.3. Percentage of Tags for Words that Include a Period

Table 4.3. Performance of Different Loglinear Models

Model	1-best Accuracy	2-best Accuracy	Residual Ambiguity
[1] [2] [3] [4] [5]	30.5%	54.4%	9.70
[12] [13] [14] [15]	55.0%	77.9%	2.73
All 2-way interactions	56.3%	86.2%	2.88
All 3-way interactions	58.2%	67.6%	2.46
All 4-way interactions	57.9%	67.9%	2.40
Saturated Model	58.1%	67.1%	2.40

features. In the model specifications, the first feature is the response variable, POS. In the absence of any other information, the ambiguity of this task is 21, corresponding to 21 equi-probable possible choices.[2]

The model assuming independent features [1] [2] [3] [4] [5] has very low accuracy. Furthermore, the high residual ambiguity for this model indicates that the model is not good at discriminating likely from less likely features. Accuracy increases as more interaction terms are added until it reaches an

---

[2] Of course, in the experiments described below, a more informative prior distribution is used that results in a baseline with lower ambiguity.

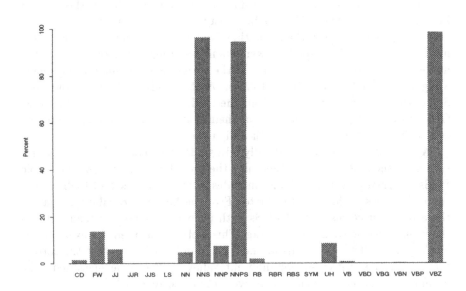

Fig. 4.4. Percentage of Tags for Words that End in $-s$

---

asymptote that corresponds to using all information that is present in the features.

The task of choosing the right interaction terms was also performed in an exploratory manner. Different models were fitted, their accuracies were evaluated, and the highest-accuracy model was determined.

4.3 Evaluation and Experimental Results

Words take on different Parts-of-Speech in different contexts. For this reason, the result returned by the model is a probability distribution over all possible POSs. For example, given a particular unknown word, the model might indicate that the word has a 60% probability of being a noun, a 20% percent probability of being a verb, and so on.

The *overall accuracy* of the model can be measured as the percentage of cases where the most likely POS is the correct answer. This corresponds to using a zero-one loss function (see Section 3.2.3 for further details). When the model is integrated with a contextual component in a POS tagging procedure, a number of possible answers can be carried along until a latter stage, and so the model can return an "answer set" instead of a single answer.

In this case, the tags in the answer set can be selected by chosing the n most likely POSs returned by the model. The actual probabilities returned by the model can also be used to determine the answer set. One method would be to choose some threshold probability, say 30%, and consider all POSs that have a higher probability than this threshold as part of the answer set. This method would result in good answer sets if the probabilities returned by the model were distributed evenly, so that the correct answer would always have a higher probability than the cutoff. In practice, this is often not the case. Some words carry a lot of clues, and the model can make a confident guess. Other words carry little indication of their syntactic identity, and the model is not able to return any POS with a high probability.

A different method automatically adjusts to the quality of the guesses returned by the model. This method uses the probability function over possible POSs returned by the model, and includes in the answer set all POSs whose probability lies within a cutoff factor F of the highest probability. That is, the answer set consists of all POSs with probabilities greater than F times the probability of the most likely tag. This method was used, for example, by [de Marcken, 1990]. With this method, the number of times that the correct tag was in the answer set for different values of F can be measured. The number of tags that were in the answer set is also reported.

So far, different ways to measure the performance of the model in terms of accuracy against external evaluation data have been discussed. There is an another quantity that can also be measured. How difficult is the ambiguity problem? In a sense, how much ambiguity is there? If the two or three best guesses, for example, are considered as the answer set, then clearly some ambiguity remains. This is called the *residual ambiguity*. As described in Section 1.2.1, residual ambiguity is measured using the perplexity of the answer set. This is further explained with the aid of an example in the next section.

4.3.1 Measuring Residual Ambiguity: An Example

Suppose unknown words can have one of four possible POSs: Noun, verb, adjective, and adverb. What is the ambiguity of an unknown word? The random variable POS has four possible outcomes. For the purpose of this example, suppose that there is no additional information about it, and a uniform distribution is used as the prior distribution.[3] In that case, each possible value has the same probability:

$$p(\text{noun}) = p(\text{verb}) = p(\text{adjective}) = p(\text{adverb}) = 0.25 \tag{4.1}$$

Thus, the prior entropy of POS is as follows:

---

[3] Again, the actual experiments use a more informative prior.

$$H(\text{POS}) = -\sum_{i=1}^{n} p_i \log_2 p_i \tag{4.2}$$
$$= -(0.25 \log_2 0.25 + 0.25 \log_2 0.25 +$$
$$+0.25 \log_2 0.25 + 0.25 \log_2 0.25)$$
$$= -(0.25 * -2 + 0.25 * -2 + 0.25 * -2 + 0.25 * -2)$$
$$= -(-0.5 + -0.5 + -0.5 + -0.5)$$
$$= 2$$

So, without a model, the uncertainty associated with POS is 2 bits. The ambiguity of POS is as follows:

$$\text{AMB}(\text{POS}) = 2^{H(\text{POS})} \tag{4.3}$$
$$= 4$$

There are 4 equally likely choices. Now, what is the contribution of the model? Given the above, the appropriate question to ask is this: How much reduction in uncertainty, and therefor reduction in ambiguity, does the model provide? To determine this, the reduction in entropy of the result returned by the model needs to be calculated. Suppose that, for some word, the model returns the following probabilities:

$$p(\text{noun}) = 0.65$$
$$p(\text{verb}) = 0.25$$
$$p(\text{adjective}) = 0.07$$
$$p(\text{adverb}) = 0.03$$

The entropy for this word is as follows:

$$H(\text{POS}) = -\sum_{i=1}^{n} p_i \log_2 p_i \tag{4.4}$$
$$= -(0.65 \log_2 0.65 + 0.25 \log_2 0.25 +$$
$$+0.07 \log_2 0.07 + 0.03 \log_2 0.03)$$
$$= -(-0.404 + -0.5 + -0.269 + -0.152)$$
$$= 1.325$$

The residual ambiguity for this result returned by the model is $2^{1.325} = 2.51$. Since the original ambiguity of the problem is 4, using the results of the model has reduced the ambiguity by almost 1.5. In practice, the external evaluation measures concerning accuracy provide a more meaningful way to evaluate different models, and they are the focus of the experimental evaluations.

When a model is evaluated it is applied many times, the average accuracy and entropy scores for the different instances are calculated at the end of the experiment, and the average ambiguity is calculated from the average entropy.

4.3.2 Results from Previous Work

To provide a baseline, some simple probabilistic models for unknown words that use only one feature, or that assume that the different features are independent, were reimplemented. The performance of the different models is measured as follows:

1. **Overall Accuracy.** Number of times the most likely POS was correct divided by the total number of evaluation instances.
2. **Overall Ambiguity.** Mean residual ambiguity for all 21 possible POSs for all evaluation instances.
3. **2-best Accuracy.** Number of times the correct POS was among the 2 most likely POS, divided by the total number of evaluation instances.
4. **2-best Ambiguity.** Mean residual ambiguity for the 2 most likely POS for all evaluation instances.
5. **0.4-factor Accuracy.** The "factor" measure refers to an answer set derived using a cutoff factor. For F=0.4, all POSs whose probability lies within a cutoff factor F=0.4 of the most likely POS are part of the answer set. 0.4-factor Accuracy is the number of times that the correct tag was within the answer set, divided by the total number of evaluation instances. The value of 0.4 for the cutoff factor was derived empirically by experimenting with different factors.
6. **0.4-factor Ambiguity.** Mean residual ambiguity for the answer sets derived using the cutoff factor F=0.4 for all evaluation instances.
7. **0.4-factor Answer Set Size.** Mean number of tags in the answer sets derived using the cutoff factor F=0.4 for all evaluation instances.

[Magerman and Marcus, 1991] describe a procedure for dealing with unknown words that only uses the relative frequencies of the open class tags: "The lexical probability given the category is the probability of that category occurring in the corpus." Table 4.4 shows how this technique performs.

[Weischedel et al., 1993] describe a model for unknown words that uses the following features, which are treated as independent:

- INFLECTIONAL-ENDING. Possible values: *ed, ing, s*.
- DERIVATIONAL-ENDING. 32 possible values, including *ion, al, ive, ly*.
- CAPITALIZATION. Four possible values: *+sentenceinitial+capital, -sentenceinitial+capitalized*, etc.
- HYPHENATION. *true/false*.

Table 4.4. Performance of Proportional POS Assignment

Answer Set	Accuracy	Residual Ambiguity
Overall	28%	7.6
2-best	53%	2.0
3-best	67%	2.9
4-best	80%	3.8
5-best	83%	4.3

The probabilities for these features were estimated directly from tagged training data. The authors state that "while these probabilities are probably not strictly independent, the approximation is good enough to make a marked difference" in POS tagging unknown words with a POS tagger that incorporates the unknown word model. This model was reimplemented using four features: POS, INFLECTION, CAPITALIZED, and HYPHENATION. The results for this model are shown in Table 4.5. (The meaning of the F-factor answer sets is explained in Section 4.3.2.)

Table 4.5. Performance with Four Independent Features

Answer Set	Accuracy	Residual Ambiguity	Answer Set Size
Overall	61%	1.7	
2-best	77%	1.5	
3-best	85%	1.6	
4-best	89%	1.7	
5-best	95%	1.7	
0.7-factor	63%	1.1	1.2
0.4-factor	66%	1.2	1.2
0.1-factor	77%	1.5	2.0
0.07-factor	77%	1.5	2.0
0.04-factor	79%	1.5	2.0

4.3.3 Constructing the Loglinear Model

A loglinear model was constructed with exactly same features as in the model of four independent features. The loglinear model contained all the two-factor interaction terms. The results for this model are shown in Table 4.6.

The model with the highest accuracy consists of two contingency tables. The first table contains the following seven features:

– POS. *CD, FW, JJ, JJR, JJS, LS, NN, NNS, NNP, NNPS, RB, RBR, RBS, SYM, UH, VB, VBD, VBG, VBN, VBP, VBZ.*

Table 4.6. Performance of the Loglinear Model with Four Features

Answer Set	Accuracy	Residual Ambiguity	Answer Set Size
Overall	69%	1	
2-best	87%	1.6	
3-best	94%	2.1	
4-best	97%	2.3	
5-best	97%	2.4	
0.7-factor	69%	1.0	1.0
0.4-factor	81%	1.4	1.6
0.1-factor	92%	2.0	2.7
0.07-factor	95%	2.2	3.2
0.04-factor	96%	2.3	3.5

Table 4.7. Performance of the Loglinear Model with Nine Features

Answer Set	Accuracy	Residual Ambiguity	Answer Set Size
Overall	73%	1	
2-best	87%	1.8	
3-best	93%	2.3	
4-best	96%	2.7	
5-best	98%	2.9	
0.7-factor	77%	1.1	1.1
0.4-factor	86%	1.6	1.8
0.1-factor	94%	2.3	2.9
0.07-factor	96%	2.6	3.7
0.04-factor	97%	2.8	4.3

- ALL-UPPER-CASE. *true/false.*
- HYPHENATION. *true/false.*
- INCLUDES-NUMBER. *true/false.*
- CAPITALIZATION. Three values: "capitalized in sentence initial position", "capitalized in the middle of the sentence", and "lower case". [4]
- INFLECTION. *ed, er, est, ing, ly, s, no-inflection.*
- SHORT. *true/false.*

The second table handles the affixes with the following features:

- POS.
- PREFIX. The 26 prefixes that occurred 100 or more times in the training data, plus a "no-prefix" value:

---

[4] Note that this feature could be improved to only hold for words over a certain length, to avoid confusion with the ALL-UPPER-CASE feature.

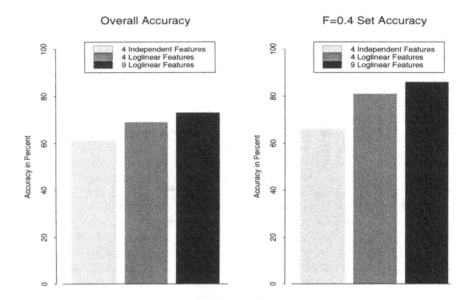

Fig. 4.5. Performance of Different Models

---

ab ac ad af ag al am an anti ap ar as at be bi co col com con cor de di dis el em en es ex for im in inter ir is mal micro mid mis non ob out over pan per pre pro re self sub super tele trans tri un under

– SUFFIX. The 37 suffixes that occurred 100 or more times in the training data, plus a "no-suffix" value:

able ade age al an ance ant ar ary ate ation ative ce ear ed ee en ent er ery es ess est ful ia ial ian ic ical ide ie ied ier ies ile ine ing ion ious ish ism ist ite ity ive ize land le line ling ly man men ment nd ness on or ous rd ry s st ster th tion ty ure us way ying

The two tables were smoothed with the [12] [13] [14] [15] [16] [17] and [12] [13] loglinear model, respectively. Then, to derive the POS probability function for an unknown word, the probabilities from the two tables were averaged, and the POS distribution was renormalized. The results for this model are shown in Table 4.7. As the table shows, there is a negative correlation between ambiguity and accuracy   answer sets with higher accuracy have a higher residual ambiguity.

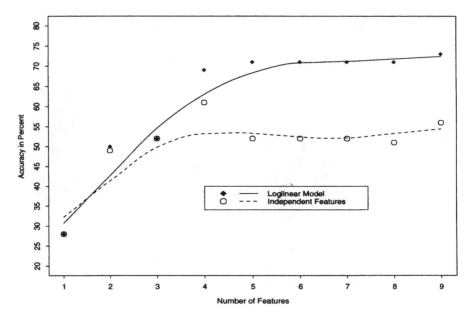

Fig. 4.6. Effect of Number of Features on Accuracy

4.3.4 Experimental Results

The accuracies of the different models are summarized in Figure 4.5. The two charts show two different accuracy measures: Percent correct, and percent correct within the F=0.4 cutoff factor answer set. Each plot compares three different models: A model combining four features as if they were independent (Table 4.5), a model using the same four features but combining them with a loglinear model, (Table 4.6), and a loglinear model using nine features (Table 4.7). In each case, the statistical method on four features performs better than the model assuming independence of the four features. The loglinear model with nine features further improves this score (except for the case of F=0.4 cutoff factor accuracy, which is a broad enough measure so that four features suffice to include as many correct tags as nine features.)

These results show a number of trends. First, on the same set of features, the loglinear method performs significantly better (8% – 17%) than a simple method assuming independence of features. Second, the performance of the loglinear method is not degraded by irrelevant features, and it can be further improved by 4% – 5% by adding features that contain additional information. (The next section shows that this is not possible with the simple model assuming independence between the features.)

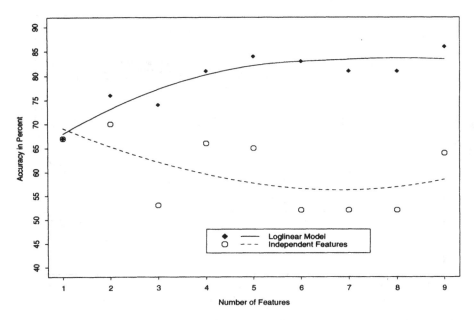

Fig. 4.7. Effect of Number of Features on F=0.4 Cutoff Factor Accuracy

---

As can be seen in Figure 4.5, there is a higher gain in switching from four independent features to the loglinear model with four features, than there is in adding more features to the loglinear model. Thus, the interactions between the four original features contribute more information than the additional features.

4.3.5 Effect of Number of Features on Performance

The previous section showed that the performance of the loglinear approach can be improved by adding more features that contain additional information. Is this also possible with the simple approach that assumes independence between the different features? In order to answer this question, the performance of the two types of models (one assuming independence of features, the other using the loglinear model) was measured with feature sets that ranged from a single feature to nine features. The accuracy for the series of models is shown in Figure 4.6.

This diagram shows that the different methods of combining features have very different effects. The accuracies for both methods rise with the first few features, but then the two methods show a clear divergence. The accuracy of the method assuming independent features levels around at around 50–55%, while the loglinear model reaches an accuracy of 70–75%.

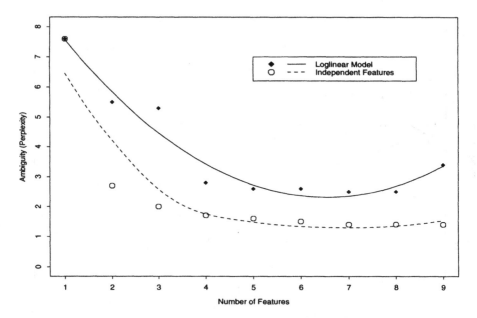

Fig. 4.8. Effect of Number of Features on Residual Ambiguity

Similar trends can be observed in the graph of feature set size versus model cutoff factor accuracy for the cutoff factor F=0.4. This graph is shown in Figure 4.7. While there is greater variability in the samples for independent features than in the samples for the loglinear method, this performance measure also shows a clear difference between the two methods. The cutoff factor accuracy for the loglinear model displays an overall rise from around 67% with one feature to 80-85% with all nine features. The cutoff accuracy of the simpler method while the simpler method actually falls from around 67% to 55-60%.

4.3.6 Number of Features and Residual Ambiguity

The accuracy of different models is an important measure, but if we consider an answer set that consists of more than the most likely tag, then other considerations come into play. How good is the returned probability distribution? In other words, how far is it from the correct answer?

As described in Section 4.3, this can be measured using residual ambiguity. The effect of feature set size on overall residual ambiguity (i.e. the residual ambiguity in the returned probability distribution over the entire set of open class tags) is shown in Figure 4.8. This graph shows that the answer set returned by the loglinear model has a higher residual ambiguity than the

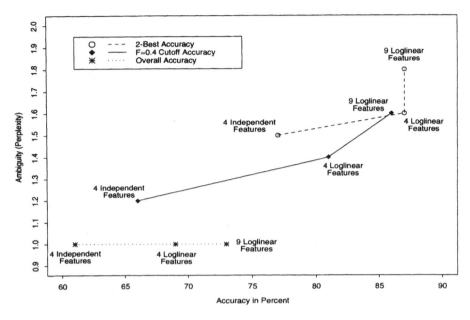

Fig. 4.9. Ambiguity versus Accuracy in Different Models

simpler method assuming independent features. The simpler method bottoms out between 1 2, while the loglinear method settles at around 2 3.

4.3.7 The Tradeoff between Accuracy and Ambiguity

What is the interaction between accuracy on one hand, and residual ambiguity on the other? Figure 4.9 shows a scatter plot of residual ambiguity versus accuracy. As the legend shows, the lines connect sets samples with the same accuracy measure. Each point in the diagram corresponds to one particular method. For example, the point in the upper right-hand corner labeled "9 loglinear features" corresponds to the loglinear model with nine features where the answer set is derived using the F=0.4 cutoff factor.

The ideal model would be located in the bottom right-hand corner, with high accuracy and low residual ambiguity. The best accuracy/residual ambiguity tradeoff depends on each application's utility function, which is very difficult to determine analytically. For this reason, the subsequent experiments rely on empirical, external evaluation of accuracy on unseen evaluation data. Chapter 5 describes experiments that integrate the loglinear unknown word model with a stochastic model of context. In particular, Figure 5.8 in Section 5.3.12 shows the error rate for the combined method on unknown words, and Figure 5.9 in Section 5.3.13 shows the overall error rate on all words.

5. Part-of-Speech Ambiguity

This chapter describes the experiments on the resolution of Part-of-Speech ambiguity. First, stochastic methods for Part-of-Speech tagging are discussed in Section 5.1. The discussion is centered around explicating the independence assumptions that underlie the common Markov model-based tagging method. Section 5.2 discusses some problems related to the estimation of contextual probabilities, and different smoothing techniques that can be employed to address the problem of sparse data. A series of experiments concerning the role of new words are described in Section 5.3. Finally, Section 5.4 describes an alternative approach to POS tagging with a loglinear model.

5.1 Stochastic Part-of-Speech Tagging

In a probabilistic framework, the problem of resolving lexical categorical ambiguity can be stated as follows: Given a sentence W consisting of a sequence of words $w_1, w_2, \ldots, w_n$, determine the most probable sequence of lexical categories or Part-of-Speech (POS) tags $T = t_1, t_2, \ldots, t_n$. We will begin by reviewing some some stochastic approximations to this problem in this section.

5.1.1 Maximizing Tag Sequence Probability

Let the sequence $T_{\max}$ be the tag sequence that maximizes the conditional probability of the tag sequence T given the word sequence W. Using Bayes rule, $P(T|W)$ can be rewritten as follows:

$$P(T|W) = \frac{P(T)P(W|T)}{P(W)} \tag{5.1}$$

The POS tagger needs to find the tag sequence $T_{\max}$ that maximizes the conditional probability $P(T|W)$. Substitution into Bayes rule yields the following:

$$T_{\max} = \mathrm{argmax}_T \frac{P(T)P(W|T)}{P(W)} \tag{5.2}$$

Since $P(W)$ does not depend on T, $P(W)$ can be dropped from this equation. Thus, the most probable tag sequence $T_{\max}$ maximizes the following quantity:

$$T_{\max} = \operatorname{argmax}_T P(T)P(W|T) \tag{5.3}$$

The tag sequence T and the word sequence W can be expanded to their constituents:

$$\operatorname{argmax}_T P(T)P(W|T) = \tag{5.4}$$
$$\operatorname{argmax}_T P(t_1, t_2, \ldots, t_n)P(w_1, w_2, \ldots, w_n|t_1, t_2, \ldots, t_n)$$

The definition of the probability of two conjoined events is as follows:

$$P(A, B) = P(A)P(B|A) \tag{5.5}$$

Therefore, the following holds:

$$\operatorname{argmax}_T P(T)P(W|T) = \operatorname{argmax}_T P(T, W) = \operatorname{argmax}_T P(W, T) \tag{5.6}$$

This can be substituted into Equation 5.5 to obtain the following:

$$\operatorname{argmax}_T P(W, T) = \operatorname{argmax}_T P(t_1, t_2, \ldots, t_n, w_1, w_2, \ldots, w_n) \tag{5.7}$$
$$= \operatorname{argmax}_T P(w_1, t_1, w_2, t_2, \ldots, w_n, t_n)$$

5.1.2 Making Independence Assumptions

There are many ways Equation 5.7 can be factored into smaller terms. In general, based on the definition of conjoined probability, the following way is used:

$$\operatorname{argmax}_T P(t_1)P(w_1|t_1)P(t_2|w_1, t_1)P(w_2|t_1, w_1, t_2)\ldots \tag{5.8}$$

This can be rewritten as follows:

$$\prod_{i=1}^{n} P(w_i|w_1, t_1, \ldots, w_{i-1}, t_{i-1}, t_i)P(t_i|w_1, t_1, \ldots, w_{i-1}, t_{i-1}) \tag{5.9}$$

The probability distributions $P(T)$ and $P(W|T)$ have far too many parameters to estimate, so some independence assumptions are commonly made. $P(T)$ is replaced by an expression that assumes that the probability of a tag only depends on the previous two tags:

$$P(t_i|t_1, t_2, \ldots, t_{i-1}) \approx P(t_i|t_{i-1}, t_{i-2}) \tag{5.10}$$

This can be thought of as a reduction of the sample space by grouping all tag histories $t_1, t_2, \ldots, t_{i-1}$ into a much smaller set of equivalence classes, depending only on the last two tags. Thus, the following approximation is used:

$$P(T) \approx \prod_{i=1}^{n} P(t_i|t_{i-1}, t_{i-2}) \qquad (5.11)$$

The conditional probability $P(W|T)$ is simplified by the following independence assumption: It is assumed that the occurrence of a word does not depend on the occurrence of any previous words, but only on the previous tag history:

$$P(w_i|w_1, w_2, \ldots, w_{i-1}, t_1, t_2, \ldots, t_{i-1}) \approx P(w_i|t_1, t_2, \ldots, t_{i-1}) \qquad (5.12)$$

Furthermore, the tag contexts are grouped into equivalence classes depending on only the current tag, so that the occurrence of a word is assumed to depend only on the current tag:

$$P(w_i|w_1, w_2, \ldots, w_{i-1}, t_1, t_2, \ldots, t_{i-1}) \approx P(w_i|t_i) \qquad (5.13)$$

This leads to the following approximation:

$$P(W|T) \approx \prod_{i=1}^{n} P(w_i|t_i) \qquad (5.14)$$

Finally, the two main independence assumptions concerning words and tags are combined. This leads to the following approximation of the probability of a tag sequence given the words sequence:

$$P(T|W) \approx \prod_{i=1}^{n} P(w_i|t_i) P(t_i|t_{i-1}, t_{i-2}) \qquad (5.15)$$

This is the quantity that is maximized by stochastic POS taggers.

5.1.3 The Tagging Algorithm

Conceptually, the path-based stochastic tagging algorithm enumerates all complete paths T for the word sequence W, and selects the path with the highest probability $P(T|W)$. The Viterbi algorithm [Viterbi, 1967] performs this in complexity linear in the length of the sentence, and polynomial (with order equal to the order of the tag scoring function) in the maximum number of POS categories per word [Foster, 1991].

The method of "path-based tagging" selects the most probable tag sequence. A variant on this scheme, called "token-based tagging", chooses the tag sequence that is composed of the most probable tags. Each tag can participate in a number of possible paths, so the tag with the highest total probability must be chosen. This can be achieved with complexity linear in the length of the word sequence with the Forward-Backward or Baum-Welch algorithm [Baum, 1972]. For each tag position i in the tag sequence T, the following is selected:

$$\text{argmax}_t P(t_i = t|W) = \text{argmax}_t \sum_{T_{t_i=t}} P(T|W) \qquad (5.16)$$

By a similar argument as shown in Section 5.1.1, this is the same as

$$\text{argmax}_t \sum_{T_{t_i=t}} P(W,T) \qquad (5.17)$$

[Merialdo, 1994] compared the two approaches to tagging and found that token-based tagging performed slightly better.[1]

5.2 Estimation of Probabilities

This section describes the main problems related to estimating the probability distributions used for POS tagging from a text corpus.

5.2.1 Tagged versus Untagged Training Corpora

The probability distributions can be estimated from a tagged corpus, or from an untagged corpus.[2] If a tagged corpus is available, the parameters can be based on relative observed frequencies. On the other hand, a Hidden Markov Model can be trained on untagged text using the Forward-Backward algorithm. [Merialdo, 1994] compared the two approaches, and found that with more than 50,000 words tagged text available, the results for frequency-based parameter estimation using tagged text were better than the HMM-based model using untagged text. Furthermore, after training on 500,000 tagged words, any application of the HMM training resulted in performance degradation.

5.2.2 Jeffreys' Estimate

Estimating probabilities $P(X)$ directly from the observed frequencies $f(X)$ does not lead to a good model of the domain under study. One particular problem concerns events that are not present in the sample, the so-called sampling zeroes. Direct estimation would assign all these events a probability of 0, even though the probability of some of these events is bigger than 0. For this reason, estimated probabilities are usually *smoothed* to remove idiosyncrasies of the sample, and to provide a better estimate of the probabilities of events in the domain under investigation.

---

[1] It is not clear whether the observed difference in accuracy represents a statistically significant difference, or a meaningful difference in practice.

[2] This is similar to the distinction between supervised and unsupervised learning.

One smoothing method is called "Jeffreys' estimate"; it amounts to adding 1 to all counts [Good, 1965]. The problem with this is that it over-estimates the events with a small probability, which probably have a small count in the sample [Gale and Church, 1994]. Word frequencies have been noted to follow "Zipf's law" [Zipf, 1949]: Looking at a frequency-ranked list of words in a text corpus, the rank of a word divided by the frequency of the word in the corpus is near constant. For example, if the most frequent word in a corpus occurs n times, the second most frequent word occurs about $n/2$ times, the third most frequent word occurs $n/3$ times, and so on. This means that most words occur at very small frequencies. Thus, Jeffreys' estimate (or "adding one") is not an appropriate smoothing procedure.

5.2.3 Linear Interpolation

The linear interpolation smoothing scheme runs as follows. Observed counts $f(x)$ are be modified by adding a floor value from a less specific distribution $q(X)$ with weight α, such as a unigram distribution [Ney and Nessen, 1991]. Then, the probability distribution is approximated as follows:

$$p(x) \approx \frac{f(x) + \alpha q(x)}{N + \alpha} \qquad (5.18)$$

The traditional interpolation parameter $\lambda = \frac{\alpha}{N+\alpha}$, so that the following approximation holds:

$$p(x) \approx (1 - \lambda)\frac{f(x)}{N} + \lambda q(x) \qquad (5.19)$$

In this scheme, each sample count $f(x)$ is discounted by the value $\lambda f(x)$. Trigram probabilities can be interpolated from bigram and unigram probabilities [Kuhn and Mori, 1990]:

$$p(w_i|w_{i-1}, w_{i-2}) \approx \lambda_2 f(w_i|w_{i-1}, w_{i-2}) + \lambda_1(w_i|w_{i-1}) + \lambda_0 f(w_i) \quad (5.20)$$

In this case, $\lambda_0 + \lambda_1 + \lambda_2 = 1$, and their values are chosen to to maximize the probability of some unseen training text. In the simplest case, the lexical and contextual probabilities can be smoothed by a linear combination with a uniform distribution [Merialdo, 1994]:

$$P(t_3|t_1, t_2) \approx \lambda f(t_3|t_1, t_2) + \frac{(1 - \lambda)}{\text{Number of tags}} \qquad (5.21)$$

$$P(w|t) \approx \lambda f(w|t) + \frac{(1 - \lambda)}{\text{Number of words}} \qquad (5.22)$$

5.2.4 Deleted Interpolation

There are a number of possible ways to set the interpolation parameter λ. The "held-out method" consists of dividing the training data into a retained part to derive the frequencies, and a held-out part to estimate the interpolation parameter.

An extension of this scheme is called the "leaving-one-out method" [Jelinek and Mercer, 1980]. The training data is divided into n blocks. Then, for $i = 1, \ldots, n$, block i forms the held-out part, and the rest forms the retained part. The interpolation parameters are estimated from block i, while the probabilities are estimated from the other blocks. This is repeated n times so that each block is considered as the held-out part once.

[Derouault and Merialdo, 1986] describe how linear interpolation parameters were estimated for the following language model, where $g(w)$ denotes the Part-of-Speech of the word w, g_{i-1} and g_{i-2} are the two preceding POSs, vocabulary size is n, e is an arbitrary floor value of 10^{-4}, and $\lambda_1 + \lambda_2 = 1$:

$$p(w_i|g(w) = g_i, g_{i-1}, g_{i-2}) \approx \qquad (5.23)$$
$$(1 - ne)f(w|g_i) \times [\lambda_1 f(g_i|g_{i-1}, g_{i-2}) + \lambda_2 f(g_i|g_{i-1})] + e$$

The training text was split into 75% retained and 25% held-out portions. The retained portion was used to derive frequency counts $f(g_i|g_{i-1}g_{i-2})$ and $f(g_i|g_{i-1})$. The interpolation parameters λ_1 and λ_2 were treated as a function of $< g_{i-1}, g_{i-2} >$ in two different ways: First, the histories $< g_{i-1}, g_{i-2} >$ were assigned to one of ten different groups depending on their frequency, so that higher frequency histories could contribute more weight than lower frequency histories. Second, the histories were grouped according to the POS g_{i-1}, based on the intuition that e.g. the POS following a function word like a determiner can be determined quite well using only the bigram, while in other cases the trigram should contribute more weight. In either case, the parameters were estimated as follows:

1. Initialize with arbitrary values such that $\lambda_1 + \lambda_2 = 1$.
2. Calculate the sums of the proportions of the two different weighted terms with the current values for $lambda_1$ and λ_2:

$$S_1 = \sum_{\text{held-out trigrams}} \frac{\lambda_1 f(g_i|g_{i-1}g_{i-2})}{\lambda_1 f(g_i|g_{i-1}g_{i-2}) + \lambda_2 f(g_i|g_{i-1})}$$

$$S_2 = \sum_{\text{held-out trigrams}} \frac{\lambda_2 f(g_i|g_{i-1})}{\lambda_1 f(g_i|g_{i-1}g_{i-2}) + \lambda_2 f(g_i|g_{i-1})}$$

3. Update the parameters by setting

$$\lambda_1 = \frac{S_1}{S_1 + s_2} \lambda_2 = \frac{S_2}{S_1 + s_2}$$

4. Repeat until the parameter converge.

5.2.5 Other Smoothing Schemes

The linear interpolation scheme discounts all sample counts equally, but it seems that higher counts should be given more weight, and smaller sample counts should be given les weight. [Ney and Nessen, 1991] describe a nonlinear interpolation scheme that achieves this, and show that their resulting language model has a lower test-set perplexity than a model using linear interpolation.

[Bahl et al., 1990a] describe an interpolation approach where the parameter λ depends on the reliability of the higher-order estimate. This is measured by the observed frequency of the higher order event. In their approach, a number k of relative frequency ranges is chosen, and values for $\lambda(1), \lambda(2), \ldots, \lambda(k)$ are estimated.

"Backing off" is a different approach that uses the higher-order probabilities if they are available, but otherwise uses the lower-order estimates [Katz, 1987]:

$$
p(w_i|w_{i-1}w_{i-2}) \approx \left\{ \begin{array}{ll} \lambda_2 f(w_i|w_{i-1}w_{i-2}) & \text{if} f(w_i w_{i-1} w_{i-2}) > 0 \\ \lambda_1 f(w_i|w_{i-1}) & \text{if} f(w_i w_{i-1}) > 0 \\ \lambda_0 f(w_i) & otherwise \end{array} \right.
\qquad (5.24)
$$

Again, the parameters λ_i are set to ensure that the probability over all the trigrams adds to 1; their values largely depend on the size of the training text; as the training set gets larger, the number of trigrams that has been seen increases.

The Good-Turing approach [Good, 1953, Nadas, 1985] smoothes observed frequencies based on the number of observed events with each frequency. In other words, it considers the number of events that were observed zero times, one time, two times, etc. Some work that uses Good-Turing smoothing is described in [Church and Gale, 1991a] and [Gupta et al., 1992].

5.3 Stochastic Tagging with Unknown Words

This section describes a series of experiments that integrate a stochastic n-gram context model with a loglinear statistical model for unknown words. The unknown word model was described in detail in Chapter 4. This section first demonstrates the shortcoming of a purely stochastic method, and then describes the results of combining the stochastic method with the statistical model. Section 5.4 discusses a series of experiments that use a loglinear context model to improve the performance of the stochastic component.

5.3.1 Experimental Data

The unknown word model was trained on 1 Million words from the tagged Brown Corpus; this is described in more detail in Chapter 4. The lexical and contextual probabilities of the stochastic component were estimated on 800,000 words of tagged Wall Street Journal texts. Then, the stochastic tagger was run in various different configurations on a series of evaluation samples, each consisting of 4,000 words of Wall Street Journal corpus.[3] Depending on the configuration, between 28 and 43 such evaluation sets were used.

5.3.2 Results from Previous Work

The stochastic tagging results that are reported in the literature are usually stated as average accuracy percentages with a precision of one or sometimes even two decimal points. These reported overall error rates are summarized in Table 5.2, and error rates measured on unknown words alone are summarized in Table 5.1. It is important to note, however, that it is difficult to make meaningful comparisons between different studies, because the results depend on a number of factors:

- The number of tags in the tagset.
- The number of words in the vocabulary.
- The difficulty of tagging problem – the distribution of the correct tags over the words, the degree of ambiguity of different words with respect to the tagset, etc.
- Soundness of evaluation methodology — for example, was the procedure evaluated on a subset of the testing data?

5.3.3 Boxplots

Since one of the points of interest in these experiments is to investigate the variance of the different strategies, different models were evaluated by collecting a large number of samples, and using boxplots to display the results.

Boxplots are useful to compare two series of experiments, since they provide a visual summary of a series of samples. The boxplot indicates the location and spread of the data, and the median dividing the data into upper and lowers halves makes it easy to estimate skewness of the data. Outliers are indicated by separate marks, and so do not interfere with the visual summary of the data. The boxplots below have the following properties:

- **Width.** The width of the boxes is proportional to the square of the number of evaluation samples for that experiment.

---

[3] The method that was used to obtain random samples is described further in Appendix C.

Table 5.1. Previous Results: Stochastic POS Tagging Error on Unknown Words

Authors	Results
[Kupiec, 1992]	24.1% error on unknown words 7.4% error on proper nouns
[Weischedel et al., 1993]	51.6% error using tritags 18% error using hyph/suffix 15% error with hyph/suffix & caps
[Brill, 1993] on WSJ	80.8% error if all unknown words are tagged as singular common nouns; 22.5% error trained on 1000 sentences 18.7 % error trained on 4000 sentences
[Brill, 1993] on Brown Corpus with Penn tags	71.7% error if all unknown words are tagged as singular common nouns; 25.5% error trained on 1000 sentences 18.7 % error trained on 4000 sentences
[Schuetze and Singer, 1994]	43% error with variable memory HMM (Using only priors)

- **Median.** The median is shown as a line across the box.
- **Box height.** The box is drawn between the quartiles. That is, the data points are arranged in a vertical line from the lowest at the bottom to the highest at the top, and the box is drawn so as to include the central 50% of the data points.
- **Whiskers.** Whiskers are drawn from the box for a distance 1.5 times the inter-quartile range (box height).
- **Outliers.** Outliers, further than 1.5 times the inter-quartile range away from the box, are shown by a separate mark.

5.3.4 Error Distribution

The experiments were performed with a stochastic trigram-based tagger that uses the Viterbi algorithm (see Section 5.1.3) to assign a sequence of tags, $T = t_1, t_2, \ldots, t_n$, to a sequence of words $W = w_1, w_2, \ldots, w_n$. The tagger maximizes the probability of the tag sequence T, given the sentence W, using the familiar approximation that was derived in Section 5.1.2:

$$\text{argmax}_T P(T|W) \approx \text{argmax}_T \prod_{i=1}^{n} P(w_i|t_i)P(t_i|t_{i-1}, t_{i-2}) \qquad (5.25)$$

In the first set of experiments, both the lexical probabilities $P(w|t)$ and contextual probabilities $P(t_i|t_{i-1}, t_{i-2})$ were derived as Maximum Likelihood estimates from 800,000 words of tagged Wall Street Journal (WSJ) articles

Table 5.2. Previous Results: Error Rates on POS Tagging

Authors	Results
[Green and Rubin, 1971]	23% overall error
[Garside et al., 1987]	10% error on ambiguous words 3%-4% overall error 6% overall error without Idiom-tagging
[Church, 1988]	Reported as "1%-5% error"
[DeRose, 1988]	4% overall error
[Hindle, 1989]	10% error on ambiguous words 3% overall error
[de Marcken, 1990]	12.7% error on LOB bigrams only 5.9% error on LOB lexical probs only 4.3% error on LOB bigram+context 4.0 % error on LOB path-based tagging
[Foster, 1991]	2.0% error for 3rd order Viterbi HMM
[Black et al., 1992]	On Lancaster Treebank: 3.03% error with HMM 2.61% error with Decision Tree On Penn Treebank: 4.57% error with HMM 4.37% error with Decision Tree
[Cutting et al., 1992]	4% error on Brown Corpus, HMM
[Kupiec, 1992]	ca. 4% error with HMM
[Brill, 1993]	5.6% error on WSJ 8.2% error on Penn Brown Corpus
[Charniak et al., 1993]	9.75% error using lexical probabilities 3.55% error using bigrams
[Weischedel et al., 1993]	3%-4% error rate on WSJ texts 5.6% error rate on terrorism texts
[Boggess III and Boggess, 1994]	12% error: neural network using last four letters only
[Charniak et al., 1994]	4.1% error: Viterbi tagger & PCFG parser
[Schuetze and Singer, 1994]	4.19% error with variable memory HMM

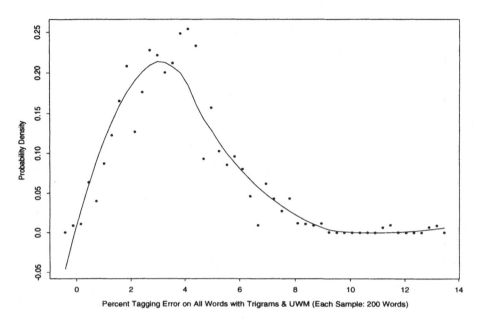

Fig. 5.1. Error Density on Samples of 200 Words

---

from the Penn Treebank. The tagger was evaluated on 30–40 test samples of 4,000 words of WSJ text.

5.3.5 Tagging Error Density

The accuracy figures that are usually reported for POS taggers represent an average over many words. But if smaller samples of tagged text are considered, how does the error vary over different samples? This question was investigated by evaluating the tagger on samples of text with different lengths, and producing probability density plots from the results. The final graph is produced by smoothing the individual data points. [4]

Figure 5.1 shows the error density graph for samples of 200 words in length. 200 words is longer than most sentences, but even with such relatively long texts there were samples with error rates over 12%. Thus, for sentences of length 20 or 30 words, the error rates vary considerably, and the error distribution is far from the Gaussian normal, with a tail extending far to the right.

---

[4] The smoothing method fits a quadratic polynomial using the Loess method. Then, the fitted model is sampled at 50 evenly spaced points, and the results are connected to form the smoothed line.

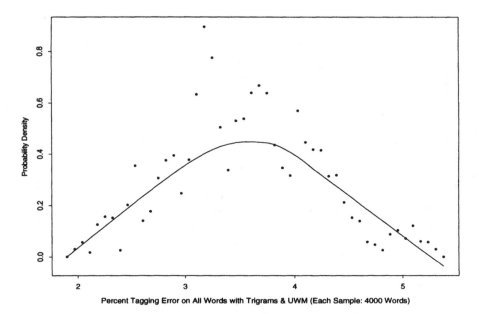

Fig. 5.2. Error Density on Samples of 4,000 words

If samples of length 4,000 words are examined, most of the long tail with high error rates disappears. But as Figure 5.2 shows, the error distribution remains more stretched out than the normal distribution, so that samples are less clustered around the median. As shown in the next section, this trend is confirmed when the error distribution is compared directly to the normal distribution.

5.3.6 Normal Probability Plot

Figure 5.3 shows the normal probability plot for samples of length 200 words. A normal probability plot provides a visual indication of whether a series of data is approximately normally distributed. The normal probability plot depends on the number of samples. A normal distribution is generated with the same number of samples, and the two distributions are plotted in a scatterplot.

Probability plots always show an increasing trend from left to right, since the samples are plotted in order. If the plot is nearly straight, then the distribution is nearly normal. In this case, the slope of the line indicates the standard deviation of the distribution.

If the plot is S-shaped, with the right part pointing down and the left part pointing up, then the variable is more stretched out than the normal

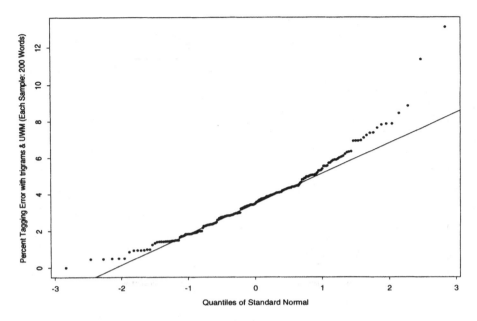

Fig. 5.3. Normal Probability Plot on Samples of 200 Words

---

distribution. If the line is S-shaped with the right part pointing right and the left part pointing left, than the variable is more compact than the normal distribution. If only one side of the line deviates from the straight line, then the variable is skewed.

As Figure 5.3 shows, the samples are more compact on the low end, and more spread out on the high end. This confirms that the error distribution is skewed to the right, which predicts more samples with significantly higher error rates than a normal distribution.

The plotted data shows a division into discrete sets because each sample only contained 200 words. This quantization effect occurs because no error corresponds to an error rate of 0% (first set); one incorrect word corresponds to an error rate of 0.5% (second set); two incorrect words correspond to an error of 1% (third set); and so on.

5.3.7 The Role of Contextual Probabilities

The lexical probability term in Equation 5.25 plays a much larger role in tagging than the contextual probability term. Figure 5.4 compares the error rates of tagging only with lexical probabilities $P(w|t)$ (i.e., choosing the most likely tag for each word), with the error rates obtained if only the trigram probabilities $P(t_i|t_{i-1}t_{i-2})$ and the lexical probabilities for closed class words

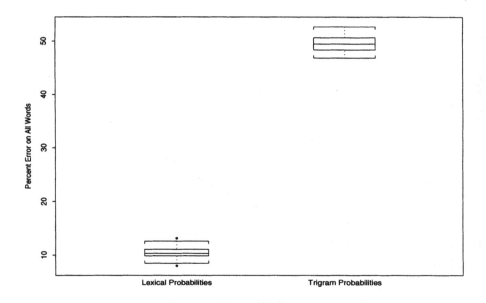

Fig. 5.4. Accuracy of Lexical versus Contextual Probabilities

(grammatical words such as determiners, prepositions, and pronouns) are used. This confirms that lexical probabilities on their own achieve around 90% tagging accuracy.

5.3.8 Bigrams versus Trigrams

Figure 5.5 compares the error rates for using $P(t_i|t_{i-1})$ and $P(t_i|t_{i-1}t_{i-2})$ as the contextual term in Equation 5.25. (A small floor value was used for trigrams that were not observed in training.) As can be seen in the diagram, *unsmoothed* trigrams actually result in a higher median error rate and greater error variance than bigrams. The reason for this is that there are many possible trigrams, and the training sample is relatively small compared to the size of this domain. Therefore, the observed trigram frequencies do not yield good probability estimates. Even though the bigrams present a much coarser picture of contextual constraints on POS sequences, there are fewer possible bigrams, so the sample space is smaller, the training sample is effectively larger with respect to the sample space, and the probability estimates are more accurate.

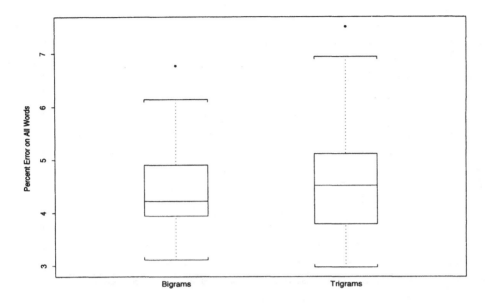

Fig. 5.5. Accuracy of Unsmoothed Bigrams versus Unsmoothed Trigrams

---

5.3.9 The Importance of Smoothing Trigrams

The higher error rate of unsmoothed trigram probabilities is due to the fact that Maximum Likelihood estimates perform badly with *effectively small* samples — situations where most events are not present in the sample. As described in Section 5.2.3, linear interpolation was used to smooth trigram counts with bigram and unigram counts:

$$p(t_i|t_{i-1}, t_{i-2}) \approx \lambda_2 f(t_i|t_{i-1}, t_{i-2}) + \lambda_1 f(t_i|t_{i-1}) + \lambda_0 f(t_i) \qquad (5.26)$$

As Figure 5.6 shows, smoothing reduces the tail of samples with high error rates, and also causes a reduction of the median tagging error.

5.3.10 Lexical Probabilities and Unknown Words

As evident in Figure 5.4, lexical probabilities play the dominant role in POS tagging. This means that words that have not been seen in training, and for which no estimates of the lexical probabilities exist, represent a serious problem.

If around 800,000 words of Wall Street Journal articles are used for training, and new text also taken from the WSJ corpus is used for testing, a rate

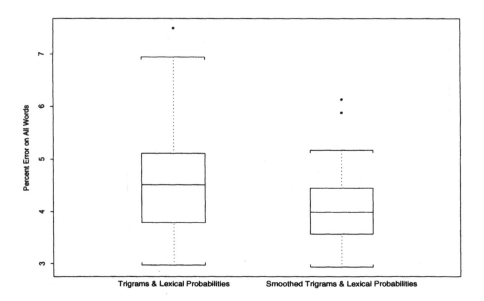

Fig. 5.6. Accuracy of Trigrams versus Smoothed Trigrams

of 2.5%–3% new or *unknown* words that are not part of the training test is obtained. But if the tagger is applied to a different type of text than the training corpus, the proportion of unknown words rises. Texts from technical fields, for example, contain a large amount of domain-specific terminology; unless the tagger is trained on text from the same domain, there will be a significant proportion of new words.

The simplest model for unknown words would be to use the prior probabilities for POS tags estimated from the training corpus. During the experiments, it became evident that there is a difference in the distribution of POSs between the corpus as a whole, and the types of words that occur as new words. Thus, the baseline is the prior unigram distribution over the open class tags in the unknown word training data.

To address the problem of unknown words, the nine-feature loglinear unknown word model that is described in Chapter 4 was used. The model produces a probability distribution over word features $\mathbf{v}$ given the POS, $P(\mathbf{v}|\text{POS}_{\text{open-class}})$, which is then used as the lexical term $P(w|t)$ in Equation 5.25.

In order to avoid overtraining on the rather homogeneous WSJ articles (i.e., to avoid picking up features that are specific to the WSJ corpus), the unknown word models described here were trained on text from the Brown

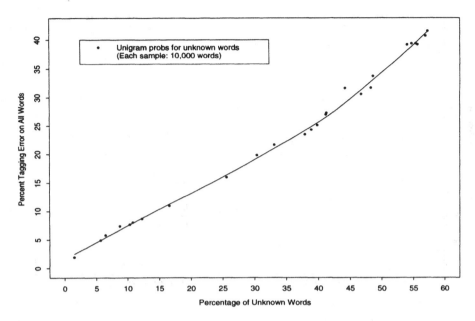

Fig. 5.7. Unknown Words and Tagging Error

Corpus. The exact procedure for obtaining training samples is described in Section 4.1.3.

5.3.11 POS Tagging and Unknown Words

In order to study the effect of tagging text that is different from the training text, a number of samples of 10,000 words of WSJ text were tagged with a stochastic POS tagger. The tagger used smoothed trigrams, lexical probabilities for closed class words that were estimated from 800,000 words of WSJ text, and lexical probabilities for open class words that were estimated from varying amounts of training text. For each sample, the proportion of unknown words in the test sample relative to the training text, as well as the tagging error, were noted. As Figure 5.7 shows, there is a clear correlation between the proportion of unknown words, and the error rate.[5]

---

[5] The graph is the result of smoothing by fitting a quadratic polynomial using the Loess method. Then, the fitted model is sampled at 50 evenly spaced points, and the results are connected to form the smoothed line.

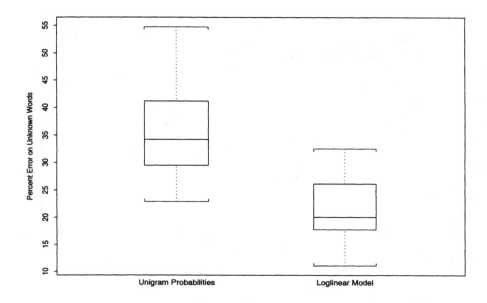

Fig. 5.8. Error Rate on Unknown Words

5.3.12 Unknown Word Model Results

Figure 5.8 compares the error rate on unknown words with contextual trigram probabilities and unigram probabilities for unknown words, with the error rate on unknown words using the loglinear unknown word model. The loglinear unknown word model eliminates all samples with over 32% error, and reduces the median error rate by about 40%.

5.3.13 Effect of Statistical Model on New Text

The reduction in errors on unknown words has a significant effect on overall tagging accuracy if the text contains larger proportions of unknown words. Three methods of handling unknown words were compared:

– **Unigram:** Using the prior probability distribution of the POS tags for rare words, as described in Section 5.3.10.
– **Probabilistic UWM:** Using a model that is based on four independent features. (This is a reimplementation of   the method described in [Weischedel et al., 1993], which assumes independence between the features. As shown in Section 4.3.5, the accuracy of this method can not be improved by adding more features.)

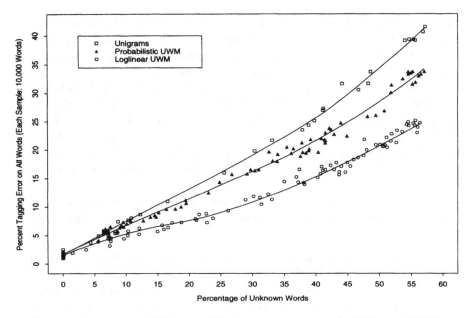

Fig. 5.9. Percentage of Unknown Words versus Accuracy for Different UWMs

---

- **Classifier UWM**: Using the loglinear model with seven features. The F=0.01 cutoff factor answer set is used to supply lexical probabilities for the stochastic POS tagger. This value was derived empirically by experimenting with a range of different n-best and cutoff factor answer sets.

While Figure 5.8 described error rates on unknown words, Figure 5.9 describes the overall error rates on all words. Figure 5.9 shows a graph of overall tagging accuracy versus percentage of unknown words. The diagram shows that the unknown word model leads to better overall tagging performance than the simpler methods, with a clear separation of all samples whose proportion of unknown words is above 10%.

5.4 Errors Analysis for the Trigram-based Tagger

The previous section described a method for POS tagging that consists of a combination of a stochastic tagging procedure with a loglinear model for unknown words. As shown in Section 5.1.2, stochastic tagging is based on some rather significant independence assumptions. This section describes an experiment that uses a loglinear model, which does not require such drastic independence assumptions, to correct the mistakes committed by the stochastic procedure.

5.4.1 Qualitative Error Analysis

From the experiments with the stochastic trigram-based tagger, it was evident that the type of error that occurred most frequently in Wall Street Journal texts concerns pre-nominal modifiers, especially those involving present participles (*-ing* forms) and past participles (*-ed* forms.)

[Kupiec, 1992] analyzed the errors made by his HMM-based POS tagger that was described in Section 2.3.3, and added states to the HMM topology to capture additional constraints, implementing a strategy of "selective choice of higher order context." Some errors were due to the equivalence-class based method for lexical states. For example, the equivalence class *adjective-or-noun* includes few nouns, and more adjectives, so this class prefers an adjective reading.

A second type of error shows the inadequacy of n-gram models. Consider the following sentences (all examples in this section are taken from [Kupiec, 1992]):

    a. Temperatures in the upper mantle range apparently from ...   (5.27)
    b. The velocity of the seismic waves rises to ...

The words *range* and *rises* were tagged as nouns, and not as verbs. Statistically, nouns are more often followed by verbs with the same number. In these examples, there is a dependency spanning the prepositional phrases. In response to these problems, Kupiec added network states for the sequence "Noun-Preposition-Determiner-Adjective-Noun-Noun/Verb." (It is not clear how many such highly specific sequences were added.)

The most frequent type of error in Kupiec's tagger was mistagging nouns as adjectives. Kupiec notes that this is partly due to their variability in order in NPs, but that sometimes semantics would be required for disambiguation, as the following examples show.

    a. He issued an executive/ADJ order.   (5.28)
    b. The primary/NOUN election has begun.

In these examples, *executive* and *primary* are categorically ambiguous between noun and adjective. Another problem is the distinction between particle and preposition. Sometimes this can be decided based on the identity of the verb, but sometimes semantics would be needed:

    a. He ran up/PARTICLE a big bill.   (5.29)
    b. He ran up/PREPOSITION a big hill.

Another type of error involves the morphological ambiguity between past tense and past participle in a reduced relative clause. Note that this distinction is a difficult one to make for people, too:

    a. The loan needed/PAST to meet the rising costs of health care. (5.30)
    b. They   cannot   now   handle   the
       loan needed/PAST-PARTICIPLE to meet the rising costs of
       health care.

5.4.2 Quantitative Error Analysis

Examining tagger output and assigning errors to linguistic categories is a useful component in error analysis, but it is also illuminating to carry out quantitative analysis. A stochastic trigram-based tagger was trained on 800,000 words of tagged WSJ text, and evaluated on 100,000 words of WSJ text. Error analysis begins with an examination of the most frequent errors committed by the tagger, ranked by the percentage of the total error. This data is shown in Table 5.3.

Table 5.3. The Ten Most Frequent Errors in Stochastic Trigram-based POS Tagging

1.	NN tagged as JJ	8.7% of all errors
2.	NN tagged as NNP	5.9% of all errors
3.	IN tagged as RB	4.7% of all errors
4.	VBD tagged as VBN	4.5% of all errors
5.	NNP tagged as NN	4.1% of all errors
6.	JJ tagged as NN	3.4% of all errors
7.	NNP tagged as JJ	3.3% of all errors
8.	NNP tagged as NNPS	3.2% of all errors
9.	VBN tagged as JJ	2.8% of all errors
10.	JJ tagged as VBN	2.8% of all errors

5.4.3 Overall Error Distribution of the Stochastic Tagger

After examining the ten most frequent tagging mistakes, the next step in the analysis is to examine how the total number of errors is divided into the different *confusions*. (A confusions is an instance of tagging a word whose actual Part-of-Speech is X incorrectly with some tag Y.) All errors that occurred four times or less were ignored; then the percentage of each individual mistake of the total error was calculated. A table containing this data can be found in Appendix D.

5.4.4 Confusion Matrix of the Stochastic Tagger

The previous section examined stochastic tagger performance from the perspective of the overall error distribution. Another way to analyze the errors is to determine the tagging accuracy within each tag. A table containing this data can be found in Appendix D.

Two tags stand out for having rather low accuracy: Plural proper nouns (NNPS) with 68% accuracy, and particles (RP) with 62%. Both of these tags occur with relatively low frequency, which leads to estimation problems due to sparse training data. In addition, particles (RP) are often confused by the tagger with prepositions (tagged IN), since it is difficult for the tagger to tell the difference between a phrasal verb, consisting of verb + particle + object, and a verb + preposition + object sequence.

5.4.5 Results of Error Analysis

Based on an examination of the results presented above, almost three-quarters of the tagging errors can be grouped into three error clusters.[6] The three clusters are as follows:

1. Proper nouns, adjectives, and common nouns (JJ NN NNP NNS NNPS). This cluster accounts for about 43% of the overall error.

   If the POS tagger is used as the first stage in a wide-coverage parser for some application, some errors are more problematic than others. Some of the errors in this cluster fall into the more problematic category. It is important for most applications to accurately distinguish proper nouns and common nouns. For example, data extraction relies heavily on identifying company and other proper names. As another example, in machine translation, actually translating personal or company names that are ambiguous with common nouns (such as *Baker*) results in rather awkward mistakes.

   This cluster also includes the error pattern involving JJ (adjective) versus NN (common noun) labeling of a nominal form that is modifying another nominal form, such as "recent/JJ record/JJ-NN level/NN".

   Some of these errors are simple confusions between singular and plural forms. But some errors involving the number feature seem to be due solely to unusual lexical conventions, such as "Hot/NNP Springs/NNP-NNPS", "Association/NNP of/IN Manufacturers/NNP-NNPS", and as such can probably be only corrected by adding these items to the lexicon.

2. Particle, Preposition/Subordinate conjunction, Adverb (RP, IN, RB). This cluster accounts for about 20% of the overall error.

   Most of the errors in this cluster correspond to different possible ways of analyzing sequences consisting of a verb, and additional closed-class word, and optionally an object. Such a sequence can be tagged as a phrasal verb consisting of a verb + particle sequence, a verb + adverb sequence, or, if there is a following noun phrase, a verb + preposition + prepositional object combination.

3. Common nouns and verbs (NN NNS VB VBD VBG VBN VBP VBZ). This cluster accounts for about 11% of the overall error.

---

[6] As pointed out by Chris Manning (personal communication), there are a number of smaller clusters that have an even higher density of confusions: (VBN, VBD), (NNS, VBZ), (NN,VB,VBP), (NN, VBG), (JJ, NN, NNP), (NNPS, NNS). However, these clusters overlap, and they would leave the confusions involving NNP and NNPS stranded.

After examining tagger output, it seems that matrix verbs are hardly ever confused with nouns. Instead, most of the confusions in this cluster involve pre-nominal modifiers. This explains why there is also a certain involvement of adjectives (JJ) in this group.

5.5 Using A Loglinear Model for Lexical Disambiguation

The traditional model for tagging (Equation 5.25) assumes independence between the lexical and contextual probabilities. The remainder of this section investigates by how much tagging accuracy can be improved with a model that does not make this independence assumption.

As with the work on loglinear modeling of unknown words described in Chapter 4, the loglinear tagging model is based on a number of premises. First, lexical and contextual probabilities are not independent. Second, there are other features that need to be considered. Third, modeling the interdependence between these features is crucial.

Based on these premises, the strategy of "tagging correction" was adopted. A stochastic tagger based on Equation 5.25 is used for an initial tagging pass. In the second, "correction" pass, each tag that falls into a confusion set is re-examined, and the optimal tag from the confusion set is assigned to it by a statistical classifier that uses a loglinear model as described in Chapter 3 above.

The experiment focussed on the adjective-noun confusion set because it accounts for more than half of all errors. Furthermore, as described in Section 5.4.5, the correct identification of proper nouns (which fall into this error cluster) is particularly important for many NLP applications.

5.5.1 Errors before Correction

For the correction experiment, the stochastic trigram-based tagger was trained on 800,000 words of WSJ text. Error statistics were collected on the "Nouns/Adjectives" confusion set. Table 5.4 shows the resulting individual error proportions, and Table 5.5 shows the corresponding confusion matrix for the confusion set.

Table 5.4. Percentage of Overall Tagging Error for Nouns and Adjectives by row.

	JJ	NN	NNP	NNPS	NNS
JJ		4.1	3.9		
NN	7.2		3.0		1.4
NNP	3.6	5.8		5.5	.3
NNPS			.6		2.8
NNS		.3	.3	4.4	

Table 5.5. Confusion Matrix: Percentages for each Tag for Nouns and Adjectives by Row

	JJ	NN	NNP	NNPS	NNS
JJ	93.0	2.2	2.1		
NN	1.7	96.2	0.7		.3
NNP	1.4	2.3	93.0	2.2	.1
NNPS			7.4	55.5	37.0
NNS		.2	.2	2.7	95.8

5.5.2 Features for Tagging Correction

After examining tagger output and analyzing the problem, a number of features that are relevant to this confusion set were identified:

- STOCHASTIC-LABEL. The label assigned by the stochastic tagger.
- LEXICAL-LIKELY-TAG. The tag that is most likely given the lexical probability, or given the loglinear unknown word model if the word has not been encountered in training.
- LEFT-OC-TAG. The lexical tag of the first open class word to the left.
- SECOND-LEFT-OC-TAG. The lexical tag of the second open class word to the left.
- LEFT-CC-TAG. The lexical tag of the first closed class word to the left.
- SECOND-LEFT-CC-TAG. The lexical tag of the second closed class word to the left.
- RIGHT-OC-TAG. The lexical tag of the first open class word to the right.
- SECOND-RIGHT-OC-TAG. The lexical tag of the second open class word to the right.
- RIGHT-CC-TAG. The lexical tag of the first closed class word to the right.
- CAPITALIZATION. Is the word capitalized? This feature has four possible values: "+sentence-initial, +capital", "-sentence-initial, +capitalized", etc.
- HYPHEN-TAG. If the word is hyphenated, this feature contains the lexical tag assigned to the last word of the hyphenated compound, chosen in the same manner as the LEXICAL-LIKELY-TAG feature.

After experimenting with these features and different interaction terms in the loglinear model that is used to smooth the observed frequencies, the model with the highest accuracy included all second-order interaction terms, and contained the following features: LEXICAL-LIKELY-TAG, LEFT-CC-TAG, RIGHT-OC-TAG, and CAPITALIZATION.

This set of features reflects the principle that a closed-class word is associated with its head word to the right. For example, determiners precede nouns, prepositions precede nouns, etc. Similarly, an open-class word might modify another open-class head to its right. For example, adjectives precede nouns.

5.5.3 Results of Tagging Correction

The loglinear model for tagging correction was trained on 800,000 words of WSJ text. This resulted in 130,000 feature vectors. The model was evaluated on 10,000 words of WSJ text. Table 5.6 shows the error proportions within the confusion set after tagging correction, and Table 5.7 shows the corresponding confusion matrix. Note that because the overall error rate has decreased, the same number of errors (e.g. 16 instances JJ tagged as NN) now shows up as a greater percentage of the total error. After correction, the "Noun/Adjective" error cluster accounts for about 40% of the total error.

Table 5.6. Percentage of Overall Tagging Error after Tagging Correction for Nouns and Adjectives by Row

	JJ	NN	NNP	NNPS	NNS
JJ		4.6	4.0		
NN	7.5		2.3		1.4
NNP	3.4	3.2		5.5	.3
NNPS			.6		2.9
NNS		.3	.3	4.3	

Table 5.7. Noun/Adjective Confusion Matrix after Tagging Correction by Row

	JJ	NN	NNP	NNPS	NNS
JJ	92.8	2.3	2.1		
NN	1.7	96.4	0.5		.3
NNP	1.3	1.2	94.3	2.1	.1
NNPS			7.4	55.5	37.0
NNS		.2	.2	2.5	96.0

5.5.4 Summary of Results

The results of the experiment on tagging correction with the statistical model are summarized in Table 5.8.
Overall, these results only show a modest improvement in accuracy. Out of 363 errors committed by the stochastic tagger, the loglinear model was able to eliminate only 15 errors.

If we examine specific areas, it becomes evident that there are some promising trends. For example, the number of errors on proper nouns was reduced from 63 to 51; a 19% improvement. Whether or not this is considered a statistically significant achievement depends on the error distribution that is assumed for the tagger. As shown in Sections 5.3.5 and 5.3.6, the error

Table 5.8. Results of Statistical Tagging Correction

Domain	No. of Errors	Errors after Correction	Error Reduction
Proper Nouns	63	51	19.0%
Common Nouns	59	56	5.1%
Noun/Adj Cluster	207	193	6.8%
All Words	363	348	4.1%

distribution of the tagger itself depends on the size of the individual samples. If we base the estimation of the distribution on rather large samples, such as 5,000 or 10,000 words each, then the resulting distribution would be close to normal. If, on the other hand, we choose samples whose size is closer to the length of an average sentence or dialog turn, the resulting error distribution would be far from normal.

In terms of a practical application, it seems that a 19% reduction in errors on proper nouns is significant. At the same time, the overall error reduction is rather small, and it took a lot of analytical and experimental effort to obtain it. In the final analysis, it does not seem as if Part-of-Speech tagging of known words can be much improved with the loglinear technique.

6. Prepositional Phrase Attachment Disambiguation

Prepositional phrase (PP) attachment ambiguity is a particularly difficult type of structural ambiguity. Section 2.5 discussed the problem of PP attachment, and showed examples of attachment to a number of different nodes in the phrase structure tree. The examples included attachment to the most recent noun phrase node, attachment to a higher verb phrase node, and attachment to a noun phrase node that was not the most recent. To recall the nature of this problem, consider example (6.1):

[Verb Phrase Adjust [Noun Phrase the beam focus] [PP with the (6.1) calibration tool]].

Should be PP *with the calibration tool* be attached to the verb *adjust*, perhaps representing an instrument for the action? Or should it be attached to the noun phrase *beam focus*, perhaps because it forms a part of it? This chapter presents a statistical model of PP attachment that use a loglinear model to combine a number of features to obtain the most probable attachment decision.

6.1 Overview of PP Experiments

As with the previous experiments, the premise of this approach is that it is necessary to combine a number of lexical and syntactic features to resolve PP attachment ambiguity. The method is based on a loglinear model, since that is a type of statistical model that is able to combine a number of categorical features. The advantage of using a loglinear model is that it takes into account the effects of *combinations* of feature values, as well as the main effects of individual feature values.

6.2 Features for PP Attachment

The first step in constructing the loglinear model is to determine a set of features that could be used to predict PP attachment. To accomplish this, sentences with PPs in the training corpus were examined, and an initial set of features for PP attachment constructed. This set included the following features:

- **PREPOSITION.** Possible values of this feature include one of the more frequent prepositions in the training set, or the value *other-prep*. The set of frequent prepositions contains the following: *about, across, after, against, among, around, as, at, before, between, by, during, for, from, in, into, like, of, on, over, per, since, through, to, toward, under, upon, with, within, without.*
- **VERB-LEVEL.** Lexical association strength between the verb and the preposition. (This is explained in detail below.) Note that this is estimated without the sort of general verb/noun skewing term that was used by Hindle & Rooth.
- **NOUN-LEVEL.** Lexical association strength between the noun and the preposition. (Also explained in detail below.) Note that this is estimated without a general verb/noun skewing term.
- **NOUN-TAG.** Part-of-Speech of the nominal attachment site. This is included to account for correlations between attachment and syntactic category of the nominal attachment site, such as "PPs disfavor attachment to proper nouns."
- **NOUN-DEFINITENESS.** Does the nominal attachment site include a definite determiner? This feature is included to account for a possible correlation between PP attachment to the nominal site and definiteness, which was derived by Hirst from Crain & Steedman's principle of presupposition minimization.
- **PP-OBJECT-TAG.** Part-of-speech of the object of the PP. Certain types of PP objects favor attachment to the verbal or nominal site. For example, temporal PPs, such as *"in 1959"*, where the prepositional object is tagged CD (cardinal), favor attachment to the VP, because the VP is more likely to have a temporal dimension.

The association strengths for **VERB-LEVEL** and **NOUN-LEVEL** were measured using the Mutual Information between the noun or verb, and the preposition. Mutual Information provides an estimate of the magnitude of the ratio between two measures:

- **Joint probability.** The probability of observing the verb or noun together with an attached PP with a certain preposition, i.e. the joint probability P(verb/noun,preposition).
- **Independent probability.** The probability of observing both the noun or verb and the PP assuming that the two events are independent, i.e, P(verb/noun)P(preposition).

The probabilities were derived as Maximum Likelihood estimates from all PP cases in the training data. That is, the probabilities were estimated as follows, were $f(x)$ is the frequency of event x that was observed in the training sample:

$$P(\text{verb,preposition}) = \frac{f(\text{verb,preposition})}{\text{Number of verb tokens}} \qquad (6.2)$$

$$P(\text{noun,preposition}) = \frac{f(\text{noun,preposition})}{\text{Number of noun tokens}} \qquad (6.3)$$

$$P(\text{noun}) = \frac{f(\text{noun})}{\text{Number of noun tokens}} \qquad (6.4)$$

$$P(\text{verb}) = \frac{f(\text{verb})}{\text{Number of verb tokens}} \qquad (6.5)$$

$$P(\text{preposition}_{\text{verb}}) = \frac{f(\text{preposition attached to any verb})}{\text{Number of verb tokens}} \qquad (6.6)$$

$$P(\text{preposition}_{\text{noun}}) = \frac{f(\text{preposition attached to any noun})}{\text{Number of noun tokens}} \qquad (6.7)$$

Then, the Mutual Information values for nouns and prepositions were computed as follows:

$$\text{MI}(\text{noun,preposition}) = \frac{P(\text{noun,preposition})}{P(\text{noun})P(\text{preposition}_{\text{noun}})} \qquad (6.8)$$

And the Mutual Information values for verbs and prepositions were computed similarly:

$$\text{MI}(\text{verb,preposition}) = \frac{P(\text{verb,preposition})}{P(\text{verb})P(\text{preposition}_{\text{verb}})} \qquad (6.9)$$

The Mutual Information values were ordered by rank. Then, the association strengths were categorized into eight levels (A-H), depending on percentile in the ranked Mutual Information values. For example, the top two percentiles of the noun-preposition Mutual Information values were assigned level A, the third through tenth percentiles were assigned level B, and so on.

6.3 Experimental Data and Evaluation

Training and evaluation data was prepared from the Penn treebank. All 1.1 million words of parsed text in the Brown Corpus, and 2.6 million words of parsed WSJ articles, were used. (It was necessary to convert the Treebank files into Lisp-readable format; this is described further in Appendix E.) All instances of PPs that are attached to VPs and NPs were extracted. This resulted in 82,000 PP cases from the Brown Corpus, and 89,000 PP cases from the WSJ articles. Verbs and nouns were lemmatized to their root forms if the root forms were attested in the corpus. If the root form did not occur in the corpus, then the inflected form was used. For example, the verb *relegate* does not occur in its uninflected form, but always occurs as the past participle *relegated*, forming the collocation *relegated to* (and few times *relegated for*).

All the PP cases from the Brown Corpus, and 50,000 of the WSJ cases, were reserved as training data. The remaining 39,00 WSJ PP cases formed the evaluation pool. In each experiment, performance was evaluated on a series of 25 random samples of 100 PP cases from the evaluation pool. (The method used to obtain random samples from the evaluation pool is described in more detail in Appendix C.) This evaluation scheme has two main advantages. First, it made it possible to experiment with different feature sets and interaction terms in the loglinear model without invalidating the results by simply maximizing performance on a fixed evaluation set.

Second, the average accuracy figures that are usually reported in the literature indicate the accuracy to which a given method will converge if repeated a large number of times. But such average figures do not indicate the variance of the method — how likely are individual outcomes to stray from the average, and how far are they likely to stray? Variance is an important consideration, since, in an application, one is concerned with the behavior of the method on rather small samples, such as individual written sentences or spoken "dialog turns". Evaluating on a series of small samples gives an indication of the variance. As in previous experiments, boxplots are again used to summarize the performance of the PP attachment procedure over a series of evaluation samples.

6.4 Experimental Results: Two Attachments Sites

As described in detail in the overview of previous work in Section 2.5, all previous work on automatic PP attachment disambiguation has only considered the pattern of a verb phrase containing an object, and a final PP. This leads to two possible attachment sites, the verb and the object of the verb. The pattern is usually further simplified by considering only the heads of the possible attachment sites, corresponding to the sequence "Verb $Noun_1$ Preposition $Noun_2$".

The first set of experiments concerns this pattern. There are 53,000 such cases in the training data, and 16,000 such cases in the evaluation pool. A number of methods were evaluated on this pattern according to the 25-sample scheme described in Section 6.3 above. The results are shown in Figure 6.1. In this figure, each boxplot corresponds to the series of accuracy results obtained with one type of attachment disambiguation strategy. The following sections describe this series of experiments in detail.

6.4.1 Baseline: Right Association

Prepositional phrases exhibit a tendency to attach to the most recent possible attachment site; this is referred to as the principle of "Right Association". For the "V NP PP" pattern, this means attaching to the noun phrase. This

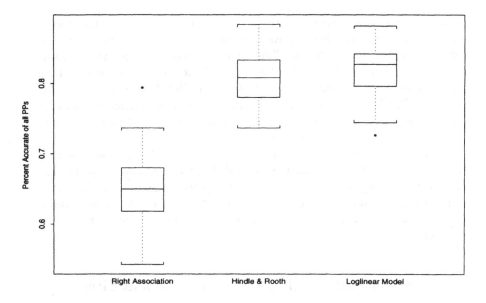

Fig. 6.1. Results for Two Attachment Sites

strategy is simple to implement, and it is used here as the baseline. On the evaluation samples, a median of 65% of the PP cases were attached to the noun. This is labeled "Right Association" in Figure 6.1.

6.4.2 Results of Lexical Association

[Hindle and Rooth, 1993] described a method for obtaining estimates of lexical association strengths between nouns or verbs and prepositions, and then using these estimates to predict PP attachment. This work is described in detail in Section 2.5.1.

The lexical association method described by Hindle & Rooth was reimplemented to provide a comparison against the loglinear method. In the reimplementation, the probabilities were estimated from all the PP cases in the training set. Since our training data are bracketed, it was possible to estimate the lexical associations with much less noise than Hindle & Rooth, who were working with unparsed text. The median accuracy for the reimplementation of Hindle & Rooth's method was 81%. This is labeled "Hindle & Rooth" in Figure 6.1.

6.4.3 Results of the Loglinear Model

Next, the loglinear method was implemented. The list of potential disambiguating features was listed above in Section 6.2. Based on this set of features, different feature sets and different interaction terms for the loglinear model were evaluated. The model that obtained the highest accuracy used the following features: PREPOSITION, VERB-LEVEL, NOUN-LEVEL, and NOUN-DEFINITENESS. The model included all second-order interaction terms in the loglinear model. This model achieved a median accuracy of 82%; this is labeled "Loglinear Model" in Figure 6.1.

As is clear from the boxplot, the results from the loglinear model are very similar to the results from Hindle & Rooth's lexical association strategy. The median for the loglinear model is about one percent higher, and the spread of the loglinear evaluation samples is a little bit less, but the overall range is very similar. Overall, there is no significant difference between the two strategies.

6.5 Experimental Results: Three Attachment Sites

On the pattern with two possible attachment sites, the loglinear method did not perform better than the lexical association strategy. But in actual texts, there are often more than two possible attachment sites for a PP. For this reason, a second series of experiments was performed that investigated different PP attachment strategies for cases with more than two possible attachment sites.

6.5.1 Additional PP Patterns

As suggested by [Gibson and Pearlmutter, 1994], the "Verb NP PP" case might be relatively easy because the two possible attachment sites differ in syntactic category, and therefore might have very different kinds of lexical preferences. This is clearly true for some prepositions. For example, most PPs with *of* attach to nouns, and most PPs with *to* and *by* attach to verbs. Thus, a more difficult problem should include two attachment sites that have the same syntactic category.

One possible pattern that fulfills this criterion would be two verbs followed by a PP, i.e. "$Verb_1$ $Verb_2$ PP". However, there are rather few instances of this pattern in the corpus. Furthermore, this pattern probably exhibits a strong tendency towards right association; that is, most PPs would attach to $Verb_2$ (Ted Gibson, personal communication). This would result in a high baseline, and would make it difficult to measure a significant increase in accuracy over the baseline.

Another possible pattern that would include syntactically homogeneous possible attachment sites is "$Noun_1$ $Noun_2$ PP". However, most cases in the

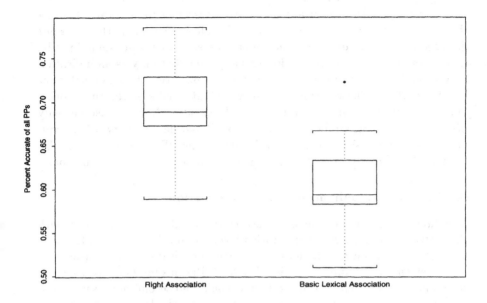

Fig. 6.2. Three Attachment Sites: Right Association and Lexical Association

corpus where a PP is preceded by two possible nominal attachment sites occur inside a verb phrase. This means that the verb should also be included as a possible attachment site. Thus, the pattern "Verb $Noun_1$ $Noun_2$ Preposition $Noun_3$" was selected for the second series of experiments. There were 28,000 such cases in the training data, and 8000 cases in the evaluation pool.

6.5.2 Baseline: Right Association

As in the first set of experiments, a number of methods were evaluated on the three attachment site pattern with 25 samples of 100 random PP cases. The results are shown in Figures 6.2–6.4. The baseline is again provided by attachment according to the principle of "Right Attachment" to the most recent possible site, i.e. attachment to $Noun_2$. A median of 69% of the PP cases were attached to $Noun_2$. This is labeled "Right Association" in Figure 6.2.

6.5.3 Results of Lexical Association

Next, the lexical association method was evaluated on this pattern. First, the method described by Hindle & Rooth was reimplemented by using the lexical association strengths estimated from all PP cases. The results for this strategy are labeled "Basic Lexical Association" in Figure 6.2. This method only achieved a median accuracy of 59%, which is worse than always choosing the rightmost attachment site. Of course, Hindle & Rooth's method was not designed for the case of three attachment sites, so these results should not be taken as a criticism of Hindle & Rooth's approach, but only as an indication that a method that only uses lexical association strength is not sufficient for this pattern. These results also suggest that Hindle & Rooth's scoring function worked well in the "Verb Noun$_1$ Preposition Noun$_2$" case not only because it was an accurate estimator of lexical associations between individual verbs/nouns and prepositions which determine PP attachment, but also because it accurately predicted the general verb-noun skew of prepositions.

6.5.4 Results of Enhanced Lexical Association

The direct application of the lexical association strategy to the pattern with three attachment sites resulted in rather low accuracy. It seems intuitive that this pattern calls for a combination of a structural feature with lexical association strength. To implement this, Hindle & Rooth's method was modified to estimate attachments to the verb, first noun, and second noun separately. This resulted in estimates that combine the structural feature directly with the lexical association strength. The modified method performed much better than the original lexical association scoring function, but it still only obtained a median accuracy of 72%. This is labeled "Split Lexical Association" in Figure 6.3, which compares three different lexical association strategies for the pattern with three attachment sites.

It is possible that the general skewing terms $\frac{f(N,p)}{f(N)}$ and $\frac{f(V,p)}{f(V)}$ used by Hindle & Rooth to smooth the lexical association estimates were overwhelming the individual lexical associations. To test this possibility, a strategy using three-way split lexical association estimates without the smoothing terms was also evaluated. This method, labeled "Split Lex. Assoc., no Skew" in Figure 6.3, performed worse than the three-way split estimation procedure, obtaining a median accuracy of 70%.

6.5.5 Results of the Loglinear Model

The relatively low accuracy of the pure lexical association strength strategy on the "Verb Noun Phrase Noun Phrase Prepositional Phrase" pattern with three possible attachment sites indicates that this pattern calls for combining structural and lexical sources of evidence.

To achieve this, various loglinear models that combine different subsets of the features listed in Section 6.2 were implemented. The highest accuracy was obtained by a loglinear model that includes the variables VERB-LEVEL, FIRST-NOUN-LEVEL, and SECOND-NOUN-LEVEL. These features use the same Mutual Information-based measure of lexical association as the previous loglinear model for two possible attachment sites, which were estimated

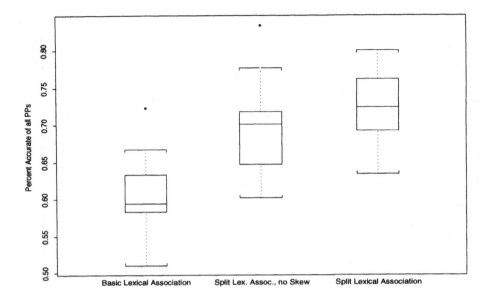

Fig. 6.3. Three Attachment Sites: Lexical Association Strategies

---

from all nominal and verbal PP attachments in the corpus. The features
FIRST-NOUN-LEVEL and **SECOND-NOUN-LEVEL** use the same estimates; in
other words, in contrast to the "split Lexical Association" method, they were
not estimated separately for the two different nominal attachment sites. The
loglinear model also includes the variables **PREPOSITION** and **PP-OBJECT-
TAG**. It was smoothed with a loglinear model that includes all second-order
interactions.

This method obtained a median accuracy of 79%; this is labeled "Loglinear Model" in Figure 6.4. As can be seen in the boxplot, it performs significantly better than the methods that only use estimates of lexical association.
Compared with the "Split Lexical Association" method, the samples are a
little less spread out, and there is no overlap at all between the central 50%
of the samples from the two methods.

6.5.6 Analysis of Results

The main results are summarized in Figure 6.4. The Lexical Association strategy with split nominal attachment site estimates does not perform well on
the more difficult pattern with three possible attachment sites. The statistical method, which uses a loglinear model to combine a number of different
features, and which provides estimates based on the *combinations* of different

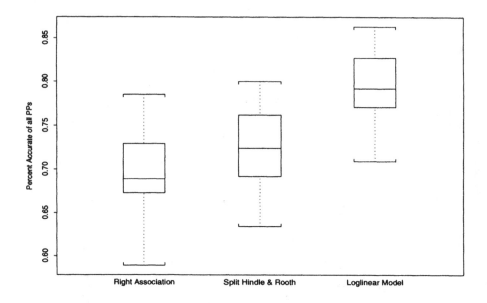

Fig. 6.4. Summary of Results for Three Attachment Sites

features, predicts attachment with significantly higher accuracy, achieving a clear separation of the central 50% of the evaluation samples.

The simpler "Verb Noun Phrase Prepositional Phrase" pattern with two syntactically different attachment sites yielded a null result: The loglinear method did not perform significantly better than the lexical association method. This could mean that the results of the lexical association method can not be improved by adding other features; but it is also possible that the features that could result in improved accuracy were not identified.

The PP attachments given in the Penn Treebank are, of course, not perfect. As noted by [Hindle and Rooth, 1993] and summarized in Section 2.5.2, there are some types of PPs for which it is not possible to identify the correct attachment site, since there is little discernible difference in meaning between different attachments. This means that in the ideal case, an automatic procedure should be evaluated only on sentences for which there is a clearly identifiable correct attachment. However, using an automatic evaluation scheme as in this work requires a large amount of manually-annotated evaluation data. If it is not possible to prepare enough evaluation data, and a corpus such as the Penn Treebank is used as the gold standard, then the target should not be 100% accuracy, but a lower figure that reflects the presence of some undecidable PP cases in the evaluation data.

6.6 Human performance on PP Attachment

There have been some studies that investigated the performance of humans on PP attachment tasks similar to the problem studied here. If random sentences with "Verb NP PP" cases from the Penn treebank are taken as the gold standard, then [Hindle and Rooth, 1993] and [Ratnaparkhi et al., 1994] report that human experts using only head words obtain 85%-88% accuracy. If the human experts are allowed to consult the whole sentence, their accuracy judged against random Treebank sentences rises to approximately 93%. Perhaps this figure could be taken as the target for automatic PP attachment procedures evaluated against random sentences from the Penn Treebank.

There has also been one study that evaluated the accuracy of the attachments in the Penn Treebank on sentences for which the human experts are able to identify a correct attachment. Starting with 300 random sentences from the Penn Treebank, [Ratnaparkhi et al., 1994] found that three human treebanking experts agreed on 274 PP attachments. Thus, the experts did not agree on almost 9% of the PP cases. Judged against the gold standard of the 274 PP attachments agreed upon by three human experts, the Penn Treebank had an error rate of 4%.

On the "Verb NP PP" pattern, the loglinear model had a median accuracy of 82%. Compared with the results of the studies using human treebanking experts, there remains an accuracy gap of 3%-6%, which remains a challenge for future work. And, if the experts are allowed to consult the whole sentence, the accuracy gap rises to about 11%. (Note that these figures should only be taken as an approximation; it is difficult to directly compare accuracy rates from different studies.)

6.7 Discussion of PP Experiments

In this chapter, we described a statistical approach to PP attachment disambiguation that is based on a loglinear model. By comparing it with the lexical association strategy, it was shown that this method is able to combine lexical and syntactic clues; this suggests that it is also applicable to other problematic types of structural ambiguity.

The results show that there is still a performance gap between human experts and the automatically trained procedure. It is likely that it is possible to raise the accuracy of the loglinear method. For one thing, the feature set could be improved by taking into account additional aspects of the context. Based on previous research on PP attachment, some possible features that could be investigated include following:

- One could attempt to identify the aspectual class of all possible attachment sites, and find a better way to identify temporal PPs.

- One could attempt to identify locative PPs, and attachment sites   that have a "locative quality" [Whittemore et al., 1990].
- One could attempt to directly implement the principles of referential success   and presupposition minimization [Crain and Steedman, 1985]. (Clearly, this would be a difficult task.)

An final point to note is that the results reported above were obtained on Wall Street Articles, which are stylistically homogeneous, but, compared to more tightly circumscribed domains, still somewhat broad in scope. The results reported by   [Ratnaparkhi et al., 1994] and [Sumita et al., 1993] suggest that our accuracy would be higher if the loglinear method was trained and evaluated on text from a more restricted domain.

7. Conclusions

We have reached the end of our exploration of the statistical approach to the problem of syntactic ambiguity resolution. In this chapter, we summarize our experimental results, draw some conclusions about automatic ambiguity resolution, and point out some areas for future research.

7.1 Summary of this Work

The following sections summarize the main results of this work.

7.1.1 Modeling Unknown Words

Chapter 4 presented the results of applying the loglinear approach to the problem of modeling the lexical category of unknown words. The chapter demonstrated that this method can help natural language analysis systems handle words that have never been encountered before.

The results show that, with the same feature set, the loglinear model performs better than the simpler method described by [Weischedel et al., 1993], which assumes independence between the features. First, the statistical method achieves higher accuracy. On the same four features, the simpler method obtained 61% accuracy, while the loglinear method achieved 69% accuracy.

Second, the statistical model handles larger feature sets, while the performance of simpler feature combination method remains lower even as more features are added. The accuracy of the statistical model can be raised by using additional features to 73%, while the accuracy of the simpler method can not be raised in the same way.

7.1.2 Part-of-Speech Disambiguation

Chapter 5 examined the performance of stochastic POS tagging. We showed that the error distribution of stochastic POS taggers is far from the Gaussian normal. This explains why, in practice, some sentences show stochastic tagging error rates that are much higher than the commonly cited average rate of 4%–5%.

Unknown words were identified as an important source of tagging error, and it was demonstrated that the loglinear model raises the accuracy on such words to a significant extent. Using the prior distribution for rare words results in a median accuracy of 66%, while the statistical model achieves a median accuracy of 80% on unknown words.

By comparing a series of samples with different percentages of unknown words (see Figure 5.9), it was shown that simpler models of unknown words bring about significantly less improvement. The results of the experiment on tagging correction with a loglinear model show that the technique can be used to improve tagging results on certain word classes. The loglinear method results in a 19% reduction of tagging error on Proper Nouns, and in a 4% reduction in overall tagging error. It is not clear, however, whether the overall reduction in tagging error is significant in practice.

7.1.3 Prepositional Phrase Attachment Disambiguation

Chapter 6 demonstrated a statistical approach to PP attachment disambiguation that uses a loglinear model to combine a number of lexical and syntactic features. Compared to the traditional AI strategy of using manually encoded semantic rules, the loglinear method has the advantage of robustness, and of avoiding the knowledge acquisition bottleneck.

On the "Verb Noun Phrase Prepositional Phrase" pattern with two possible attachment sites that have a different syntactic category, the accuracy of the loglinear method was not significantly different than the strategy of lexical association described by [Hindle and Rooth, 1993].

A second set of experiments concerned the pattern of "Verb Noun Phrase Noun Phrase Prepositional Phrase", which has three possible attachment sites, including two sites that have the same syntactic category. As [Gibson and Pearlmutter, 1994] suggested, we showed that this is a much more difficult problem than two syntactically heterogeneous possible attachment sites. The original lexical association strategy did not perform well on this pattern, with a median accuracy of only 59%. A modified version of lexical association raised accuracy to a median of 72%, but the loglinear model achieved a median accuracy of 79%.

7.2 Contributions of this Work

This section discusses this work in a wider context, and summarizes what we believe to be our main accomplishments.

7.2.1 Automatic Natural Language Ambiguity Resolution

The types of ambiguity addressed in this work constitute serious problems for any natural language analysis systems. This work provides a new technique that could help achieve the goal of robust parsing of unrestricted text.

This work has addressed a number of individual ambiguity problems from the point of view of statistical modeling. In each case, specific sets of potential disambiguating features were presented, and, following an empirical exploratory approach, sets of "core" features that contributed the most information were identified. As a result, a number of models were presented that led to higher ambiguity resolution accuracy than previously published methods. We expect that this will benefit research in computational linguistics and natural language processing that requires the ability to parse open-ended text, such as information retrieval, data extraction, text summarization, machine translation, and others.

7.2.2 Statistical Language Modeling

Throughout this book, we have also addressed the problem of statistical modeling of natural language. Statistical analysis of natural language results in *categorical* data, and we demonstrated a modeling strategy that is suitable for such data.

The loglinear method has a number of advantages over simpler modeling techniques. First, it provides a way of combining several categorical statistical variables while taking into account the interactions between the features. The modeler is not forced into making unfounded (and quite probably unsound) independence assumptions.

Second, due to the diversity of language, and the dearth of available online language data, all statistical approaches to natural language have to face the problem of sparse data. The statistical method described in this work provides a solution to this problem because loglinear models smooth the observed frequencies via the marginal totals that are specified in the model.

Third, the parameter estimation method for loglinear models results in Maximum Likelihood estimates for multinominal and independent Poisson sampling schemes.[1] Thus, assuming a multinomial sampling scheme, using a loglinear model results in optimal probability estimates.

7.2.3 Towards a Theory of Ambiguity

We believe that the experimental data presented in this book has an important implication for the theory of natural language ambiguity. Our results show that ambiguity resolution procedures that take into account the interactions between disambiguating features obtain higher accuracy than those procedures that assume independence. Therefore, we conclude that an effective ambiguity resolution strategy - whether it be implemented by man, or by

---

[1] It should be noted that the multinomial distribution might not be appropriate for natural language data, since words are clearly not independent of each other, and the multinomial model fails to account for co-occurrence effects.

machine – must account for these interactions. The details of this argument are as follows.

We have has presented a number of experiments concerning specific instances of natural language ambiguity. For each instance, a statistical model has been presented that includes the following:

- A specific set of linguistic features (or statistical variables).
- Experimental results that show higher accuracy than models that assume independence between the linguistic features.

These results provide both positive and negative evidence regarding the theory of natural language ambiguity. The positive evidence consists of showing that automatic ambiguity resolution can benefit from using the techniques employed in the loglinear method to combine a number of linguistic features. The negative evidence consists of showing that in our studies, the simpler methods were not sufficient to obtain as high an accuracy in automatic ambiguity resolution as the loglinear method. In a sense, each experiment represents a challenge to a potential theory of ambiguity: Any such theory must yield results that are comparable or better to the results from the loglinear method.

The force of the negative evidence depends on the experimental results presented in the body of this work. In each case, care has been taken to precisely implement a previously described, simpler method for ambiguity resolution; and thorough comparison of the results has shown that the loglinear method indeed yields better results for most cases.

How could the negative evidence against simpler theories be strengthened? Out of necessity, the experiments were limited to using the natural language corpora that are currently available. But the Brown Corpus and the Wall Street Journal texts are clearly not representative of the wide variety that is evident in the use of language by humans. To begin with, *spoken* language has not been considered at all. Even within the universe of written text, the Brown Corpus is simply too small to cover all varieties of written language, and the Wall Street Journal articles represent a narrow, highly specialized genre of written language. Thus, the evidence against simpler theories could be strengthened by performing additional experiments on different types of language data.

7.3 Future Work

The research presented in this work could be extended in a number of areas. First, we could attempt to improve the specific models that were presented by using additional features, and perhaps by taking into account higher-order features. Second, we could apply our method to other types of natural language ambiguity. Third, we could use this method to rank overall parse quality for entire sentences. These ideas are described in more detail below.

7.3.1 Improving the Models

Our results are promising, but it is possible that the performance of the models could be improved. The features that were used were limited to those that can be automatically extracted from the available text corpora. In the future, it is likely that text corpora will become available that have been annotated with more information. This might allow the use of additional features that result in even better ambiguity resolution accuracy. Human experts always show improvements in their accuracy when they are given additional context. For example, on the PP attachment tasks, human experts raised their accuracy by 5%-8% when they were shown the whole sentence, instead of just the head words. In the same way, the statistical model ought to obtain higher accuracy when it is given more context.

The models could perhaps also be improved by adding features that contain more linguistically significant information. For example, Section 6.7 lists a number of linguistic features that might improve performance on the problem of prepositional phrase attachment disambiguation.

Like every corpus-based approach to natural language, this work is also subject to the problem of sparse data. It is likely that the performance of the statistical models would be improved somewhat if larger text corpora were available, but, due to the distribution of words and sub-word linguistic features, the benefits derived from a larger corpus grow much more slowly than the size of the corpus itself. In particular, as we mentioned in Section 5.2.2, it has been observed that language data follows "Zipf's law" [Zipf, 1949], with the consequence of large amount of events with very small observed frequencies, no matter how large the corpus.

7.3.2 Application to other Ambiguity Problems

This work has argued that automatic ambiguity resolution requires the integration of morphological, lexical, syntactic, collocational, semantic, and pragmatic features of natural language expressions. A loglinear model provides a method for combining such categorical features, so a natural extension of the present work would be to apply it to other types of ambiguity.

Coordinate constructions represent a difficult type of ambiguity. Previous research has shown that the proper interpretation of coordinate constructions needs to take into account factors such as syntactic parallelism of conjuncts, lexical and semantic parallelism of conjuncts, and others. Using the methodology presented here, a statistical model could be constructed that predicts the likelihood of different interpretations of a coordinate construction.

Word-sense ambiguity is another difficult problem for applications that require semantic interpretation, such as Machine Translation. The approach described by [Bruce and Wiebe, 1994b] and [Bruce and Wiebe, 1994a] uses decomposable models, a subclass of loglinear models, to perform word-sense ambiguity resolution. The work uses morphological, collocational, and Part-of-Speech features to predict the sense tag from Longmans Dictionary of Contemporary English. This resulted in a 7%-9% improvement in accuracy over previous methods.

Prepositional phrase attachment is only one type of modifier attachment ambiguity. Adverbials, relative clauses, infinitival complements, appositives, and other syntactic constructions present similar problems. Syntactic rules underdetermine the correct structure, and other aspects of the sentence or utterance need to be taken into account. Similar to the case of prepositional phrase attachment that we investigated, these constructions are also natural candidates for a statistical model to predict the most likely attachment.

[Church and Gale, 1991b] describe a probabilistic approach to the problem of spelling correction. The model is based on probabilities for deletion, substitution, insertion, and reversal of letters. In addition, word n-grams are used to provide a simple model of context. As the authors state in [Gale and Church, 1990], it would be interesting to try to combine these variables with a "more sophisticated statistical approach [...] One might try to fit a log linear model."

A number of recent publications have described the use of preference score functions to rate the overall "goodness" of a parse or interpretation of a sentence, based on a number of aspects of the sentence. For example, [Chang et al., 1992] described the "Generalized Probabilistic Semantic Model". The model assigns an overall score based on lexical, syntactic, and semantic features; each feature is treated with a probabilistic scoring function. [Alshawi and Carter, 1994] describe another approach where about 20 different scoring functions are combined to provide a ranking for different semantic analyses of sentences. The different scoring functions concern features such as Right Attachment, semantic collocations, and particular syntactic configurations, such as preferring a word like *Tuesday* as an adverbial over a noun-noun compound. The different scoring functions are combined with a linear function whose parameters are estimated using regression and subsequent refinement via hill-climbing.

In both cases, the underlying problem is how to combine a number of inherently categorical features. The strategy of first constructing individual ad-hoc numeric scoring functions, and then combining the different numeric scores in some manner, introduces a number of independence assumptions that might not be warranted. An alternative approach would be to fit a loglinear model directly to the linguistic features, following the methodology that we have described.

7.3.3 Integration with Other Knowledge Sources

Under the approach presented here, "manual" expertise is used to identify features that are relevant to a problem, and an automatic estimation technique is used to construct an optimal statistical model of the phenomenon under question.

Even though the loglinear models have shown improvement over previous work, they have not been able to reach the level of accuracy attained by human experts. After performing the experiments and analyzing the errors committed by the models, my intuition is that it will not be possible to raise the performance of an automatically trained procedure to the level of human experts. This means that if high accuracy is required, it will be necessary to find robust ways of combining automatically optimized statistical models with domain-specific human expertise. This topic is sure to remain a focus for future research in statistical natural language processing.

7.3.4 Costs and Benefits of Loglinear Ambiguity Resolution Models

Constructing a loglinear model for ambiguity resolution requires a significant effort. First, relevant data needs to be analyzed by an expert, and potential disambiguating features need to be identified. Then, by means of experimentation,[2] the features that result in the highest ambiguity resolution accuracy need to be identified. The table with the smoothed cell counts, which is used to predict the probability distribution over the response variable, can have a large size; this could also be an issue for some applications.

As shown by the results presented here, a loglinear model usually offers higher accuracy than simpler ambiguity resolution procedures. Significant differences have been shown in this work by diagrams that compare series of samples. But the true test of *practical significance* will come from using models of the type described here in natural language processing applications. The best tradeoff between modeling effort and accuracy depends on the needs of the individual applications. For example, if the aim is to annotate text with POS speech labels, and there is enough similar training data to keep the percentage of new words below 2%-3%, then the gain from a loglinear unknown word model might not be worth the additional effort. Similarly, if the application did not require the highest accuracy possible, it might not be worth the effort required to construct a detailed statistical model. Conversely, if the problem was amenable to significant improvement from a loglinear model, and the task required high accuracy, then the additional effort might pay off.

7.4 Towards a Unified Model

Having progressed to the final section of this book, the reader would be forgiven for being left with an impression of a series of different experiments

---

[2] Alternatively, if training corpora of a sufficient size became available, automatic procedures for model selection could be employed.

that produced an overwhelming array of experimental results. As a final note, let us articulate one possibility for tying the different strands of this work into a unified model of natural language ambiguity resolution.

In this work, we have created individual models for each type of ambiguous natural language construction. This raises a question about how to apply this approach to ambiguity resolution in general – it might not be practical to create individual models for each type of syntactic ambiguity.

We believe that carrying out additional experiments of the sort reported here will eventually lead to the isolation of a set of general, common features that are useful across a wider range of constructions. There are already a number of candidates for this set, such as Right Association, and lexical associations strengths (perhaps measured via Mutual Information). Once such a general set has been identified, it will be possible to construct a general statistical model of how these features interact to determine the interpretation of ambiguous expressions.

A. Entropy

Entropy is a statistical measure that was originally used in statistical thermodynamics to measure disorder in a physical system. Subsequently, entropy was adopted by Shannon in Information Theory as a measure of uncertainty. Entropy is measured in *bits*. The unit for entropy is chosen so that the answer to a well-chosen yes-no question bears exactly one unit of information. For example, a random variable with two equally likely outcomes, like a fair coin, has an entropy of 1 bit.

Formally, entropy is defined as follows. Given a random variable R with n possible values with probabilities $P(R = r_1) = p_1, P(R = r_2) = p_2, \ldots, P(R = r_n) = p_n$, the entropy of R, $H(R)$, is defined as follows:

$$H(R) = -\sum_{i=1}^{n} p_i \log_2 p_i \qquad \text{(A.1)}$$

Entropy has a number of noteworthy properties. First, it can be added, subtracted, and averaged with the proper results; for example, the joint entropy of two independent random variables is the sum of the individual entropies. Second, the entropy of a random variable depends only on the number of possible values, and the probability function over the values. Third, the entropy of a random variable is highest when all possible values are equally likely, and becomes lower when some values are more likely than others. For further details, see, for example, [Ash, 1965] or [Cover and Thomas, 1991].

B. Penn Treebank Tags

This Appendix shows the Part-of-Speech tags used in the Penn Treebank. For further details on the Penn Treebank, see [Marcus et al., 1993].

Tag	Part of Speech	Example
CC	Coordinating Conjunction	and, or, but, plus, minus
CD	Cardinal Number	one, two
DT	Determiner	a, the, every, some, that those, all
EX	Existential there	There was silence.
FW	Foreign word	Fahrvergnügen
IN	Preposition, subordinating conjunction	for, on, by
JJ	Adjective	yellow, large
JJR	Comparative Adjective	larger, nicer
JJS	Superlative adjective	largest, nicest
LS	List item marker	1. ..., a) ...
MD	Modal verb	can, could, may, must, will
NN	Singular or mass noun	water, rock
NNS	Plural noun	rocks, cars
NNP	Singular proper noun	English, NATO, Nicholas March
NNPS	Plural proper noun	The *English*
PDT	Predeterminer	*all* his books, *both* his dolls *half* his time
POS	Possessive ending	John/NNP 's/POS
PP	Personal pronoun	I, me, him, myself, mine
PP$	Possessive pronoun	my, your, his, our
RB	Adverb	quickly, quite, too, very enough, not
RBR	Comparative Adverb	more, less
RBS	Superlative adverb	most, least, best
RP	Particle	on, out, by
SYM	Symbol	%, *
TO	The word *to*	
UH	Interjection	uh, hmpf

Continued on next page...

...continued from previous page.

Tag	Part of Speech	Example
VB	Base form verb	do, go
VBD	Past tense verb	did, went
VBG	Present participle verb	doing, going
VBN	Past participle verb	gone, flown
VBP	Non-3sg present verb	do, go
VBZ	3sg present verb	does, goes
WDT	Wh-determiner	which, that
WP	Wh-pronoun	what, who, whom
WP$	Possessive wh-pronoun	whose
WRB	WH-adverb	how, where, why
.	Sentence-final punctuation	. ? !
:	Mid-sentence punctuation	;
,	Comma	
"	Simple double quote	
$	Dollar sign	
#	Hash sign	
‘	Left single quote	
’	Right single quote	
“	Left double quote	
”	Right double quote	
(	Left parenthesis of any kind	({ [¡
)	Right parenthesis of any kind	) }] ¿

C. Obtaining Random Samples

This appendix describes the mechanism used to obtain random samples from the text corpus for the purpose of training and evaluation. There are three steps:

1. **Indexing.** An index of the corpus that contains counts of the relevant entities is prepared. For the experiments concerning lexical data, this index contains counts of words and sentences. For the Prepositional Phrase experiments, the index contains counts of the different types of PP cases.
2. **Storing.** The index is stored in a Lisp array, and the array with the data is stored in a compiled file. This makes it easy to reload the index for subsequent experiments.
3. **Selection.** To select random samples, the following Common Lisp function calls are used:

```
(setq *random-state* (make-random-state t))
(random *array-length*)
```

Below are two examples. The first function call selects 50,000 PP cases of any configuration from the WSJ corpus, and marks the selected PP cases with the symbol TRAIN, to note that they are part of the PP training corpus.

```
(select-pp-files :pps 50000
                 :type-to-select '(WSJ)
                 :color-selected 'TRAIN)
```

The next function call selects 400,000 words of text from the tagged Brown corpus, and marks the selected data with the symbol UWM-S1, to note that they are part of Set 1 of the unknown word model training data:

```
(select-treebank-files :words 400000
                       :type-to-select '(BROWN)
                       :color-selected 'UWM-S1)
```

D. Confusion Matrices for POS Tagging

This Appendix shows the confusion matrices for the tagging experiments described in Sections 5.4.3 and 5.4.4 of Chapter 5.

Table D.1 shows the correct tag in each row, and the tags assigned by the stochastic tagger in each column. For example, the entry "1.1" in row IN, column DT means that the mistake of labeling a word of category IN (preposition/conjunction) with the incorrect tag DT (determiner) accounted for 1.1% of the total error.

Table D.1. Percentage of Overall Stochastic Tagging Error by Row

Tagger→ Correct ↓	DT	IN	JJ	NN	NNP	NNPS	NNS	RB	RP	VB	VBD	VBG	VBN	VBP	VBZ
DT		.8						.7							
IN	1.1		.2					4.7	1.4						
JJ		.2		3.3	2.1		.2	1.7		.3	.2	.7	2.7		
NN			8.7		5.9		.4	.8				1.9	.2	.3	
NNP	.3	.2	3.3	4.1		3.2	.7	.2		.2				.2	
NNPS					1.8		1.3								
NNS			.4	.7	.6	1.1									1.4
RB	.2	2.2	2.0	.5					1.1						
RP		1.3						.7							
VB			.2	1.2									.2	1.5	
VBD		.3											4.4		
VBG			1.1	2.0											
VBN		2.8									2.6				
VBP			.2	.7						1.6	.2				
VBZ							1.3								

Table D.2 on the next page shows the confusion matrix for the stochastic trigram-based tagger. The correct tags are shown in the rows; the tags assigned by the tagger are shown in the columns. So, for example, the row for DT (determiner) shows that 99.4% of the determiners were tagged correctly, 0.3% were tagged incorrectly as IN (preposition/conjunction), and 0.3% were tagged incorrectly as RB (adverbs).

Table D.2. Confusion Matrix: Percentages for Each Tag by Row

Tagger→ / Correct↓	DT	IN	JJ	NN	NNP	NNPS	NNS	RB	RP	VB	VBD	VBG	VBN	VBP	VBZ
DT	99.4	.3						.3							
IN	.4	97.5						1.5	.5						
JJ		.1	93.9	1.8	1.1		.1	.9		.1	.1	.4	1.5		
NN			2.2	95.5	1.5		.1			.2		.4		.1	
NNP	.1		1.1	1.3	96.9	1.0	.2								
NNPS					18.2	67.9	13.1								
NNS			.2	.4	.3	.6	97.8								.7
RB	.2	2.4	2.2	.6				93.2	1.2						
RP		24.7	1.1					12.6	61.5						
VB			.3	1.4						96.0			.2	1.9	
VBD			.3								94.6		4.8		
VBG			2.5	4.4								93.0			
VBN			4.6								4.3		90.6		
VBP			.4	1.9						4.2				92.9	
VBZ							2.0								97.8

E. Converting Treebank Files

In order to be able to operate on the parsed corpus files using Common Lisp functions, the parsed Treebank files were converted into a Lisp-readable format. This was accomplished with the following Perl script:

```perl
#!/usr/misc/bin/perl

# Purpose: Iterate over Penn Treebank "combined" files,
# and rewrite in Lisp-readable format.

$brown_orig_dir = '/lusulu/usr/amf/corpora/treebank/LDC-CD-ROM/
                                        COMBINED/BROWN/';
$wsj_orig_dir = '/lusulu/usr/amf/corpora/treebank/LDC-CD-ROM/
                                        COMBINED/WSJ/';

@wsj_dir_list = ('00','01','02','03','04','05','06','07','08','09','10',
                 '11','12','13','14','15','16','17','18','19','20',
                 '21','22','23','24','25');

@brown_dir_list = ('CA','CB','CC','CD','CE','CF','CG','CH','CJ',
                   'CK','CL','CK','CL','CM','CN','CP','CR');

&reformat_brown;

&reformat_wsj;

sub reformat_brown {
    while (@brown_dir_list) {
        $brown_dir = shift @brown_dir_list;
        print "Doing Brown dir $brown_dir\n";
        @brown_files = split(/\n/,`ls "$brown_orig_dir$brown_dir"`);
        # iterate over brown files
        while (@brown_files) {
            $brown_file = shift @brown_files;
            &reformat("${brown_orig_dir}${brown_dir}/${brown_file}");
        }
    }
}
```

```perl
sub reformat_wsj {
    while (@wsj_dir_list) {
        $wsj_dir = shift @wsj_dir_list;
        print "Doing WSJ dir $wsj_dir\n";
        @wsj_files = split(/\n/,`ls "$wsj_orig_dir$wsj_dir"`);
        # iterate over wsj files
        while (@wsj_files) {
            $wsj_file = shift @wsj_files;
            &reformat("${wsj_orig_dir}${wsj_dir}/${wsj_file}");
        } # end while wsj_files
    }
}

# The subroutine reformat(infile) goes through the parse trees
# in the infile, and writes them out in Lisp-readable format
# in the Lisp readable combined files directory tree.

sub reformat {
    $infile = $_[0];
    ($outfile = $infile) =~ s/COMBINED/combined-lisp/;

    # read in entire file
    $/ = "\n\n\n";

    # allow multi-line matches
    $* = 1;

    open(INFILE,$infile) || die "Can't open input file: $1\n";
    open(OUTFILE,"> $outfile") || die "Can't open output file: $1\n";

    # action
    while (<INFILE>) {

        # skip over structures that are not parse trees
        if (/\(/) {
            # delete final spaces
            s/ *$//g;
            # collapse multiple empty lines into two lines
            s/^\n\n\n*/\n\n/g;
            # fix stray opening parens
            if (s/\n\n\(\n\n\n/\n\n/g) {
                print "Fixed stray open paren in $infile\n";
            }
            # escape existing double quotes and symbol bars
            s/([\"\|])/\\\1/g;
            # put string quotes around words
            s/ ([^\s\(\)]+)\)/ \"\1\"\)/g;
            # put symbol bars around POS tags
            s/\(([^ \n\(\)]+)([ \n\)])/\(|\1|\2/g;

            print OUTFILE ;
            print OUTFILE "\n";
            close(INFILE);
```

```
            close(OUTFILE);
        } # end if
    } # end while
} # end sub
```

F. Input to and Output from the Estimation Routines

This Appendix describes the interface between S-PLUS and Common Lisp. Most of the programs for this work were written in Common Lisp. For the estimation of our statistical models, the statistical software package S-PLUS [Statistical Sciences, Inc., 1991a] and [Statistical Sciences, Inc., 1991b] was used. S-PLUS is based on the S language [Becker et al., 1988] and [Chambers and Hastie, 1992] developed at AT&T Bell Laboratories.

The interface from S-PLUS to COMMON LISP is based on functions from CL-TO-S, a package written in 1988 by R. W. Oldford of the University of Waterloo to call S (a precursor to S-PLUS) from Common Lisp. CL-TO-S was obtained from STATLIB, an archive of statistical software, papers, datasets, and mailing list digests. STATLIB is maintained by Mike Meyer at Carnegie Mellon University, and can be accessed at http://www.stat.cmu.edu.

There are two data formats that are used for the input from Common Lisp to the iterative estimation routines, and for the output from S-PLUS back to Lisp. Data flows from Common Lisp to S-PLUS in the format of a data frame, which is a data type built into S-PLUS. Lisp writes a data frame file in the appropriate format, and S-PLUS reads the data frame with a function call similar to the following:

```
> wordfeatures <- read.table("word-features.dfm, header=T)
```

The next page shows an excerpt of the dataframe file word-features.dfm:

```
allupcase finperiod comma hyphen number inclperiod caps inflection
  prefix suffix short tag
T F F F T T lcaps no-inflection no-prefix no-suffix F CD
F F F F F F sentmiddlecaps no-inflection no-prefix no-suffix F NNP
F F F F F F lcaps no-inflection no-prefix no-suffix F NN
F F F F F F lcaps ed no-prefix ed F VBN
F F F T F F lcaps no-inflection non ment F JJ
F F F T F F lcaps no-inflection non no-suffix F JJ
F F F T F F lcaps ed ad ed F JJ
F F F T F F lcaps no-inflection no-prefix le F JJ
F F F T F F lcaps ed ad ed F JJ
F F F F F F lcaps s no-prefix s F NNS
F F F T F F lcaps er no-prefix ster F NN
F F F T F F lcaps no-inflection no-prefix no-suffix F NN
F F F T F F lcaps ing ad ing F NN
F F F T F F lcaps ed ad ed F JJ
F F F T F F lcaps ed no-prefix ed F JJR
F F F F F F sentmiddlecaps er no-prefix er F NNP
F F F F F F lcaps s no-prefix s F NNS
F F F F F F lcaps s no-prefix es F NNS
F F F F F F lcaps s no-prefix s F NNS
F F F F F F lcaps no-inflection no-prefix no-suffix F NN
```

After estimation, the smoothed contingency table is written out to data files with a function call similar to the following:

```
> write.loglin.table.to.lisp.dump(fit, "fit",
"/usr2/amf/data/pp/vpnp.allresponse.dimnames",
"/usr2/amf/data/pp/vpnp.allresponse.data.dump")
```

The function write.loglin.table.to.lisp.dump is shown on the next page.

```
"write.loglin.table.to.lisp.dump"<-
function(table, fitname, dimfile,datafile)
{
        CL.clobber.file(dimfile)
        CL.clobber.file(datafile)

        # write out dimensions of the big table
        cat("\n(setq *cont-table-dims*\n '(",
            file = dimfile, append = TRUE)
        for(i in dim(table)) {
                cat(i, ' ',  file=dimfile, append= TRUE)}
        cat('))\n\n', file=dimfile, append=TRUE)

        # write out dimension names
        cat("(setq *cont-name-list*\n\n", file = dimfile,
            append = TRUE)
        CL.write.val(dimnames(table), file = dimfile)
        cat("\n)\n", file = dimfile, append = TRUE)

        # write cell entries of big table to datafile
        data.dump(fitname,datafile)
}
```

This results in two files. The first file, with extension .dimnames, contains the names that serve as indices into the table; it is loaded directly into Lisp. A formatted example is shown below.

```
(setq *cont-table-dims*
 '(21  2  3  2  7  2  2 ))

(setq *cont-name-list*
      (list
      (cons
       (quote tag)
       (make-array
        21
        :element-type 'string
        :initial-contents
        (list "CD" "FW" "JJ" "JJR" "JJS" "LS" "NN" "NNP"
              "NNPS" "NNS" "RB" "RBR" "RBS" "SYM" "UH"
              "VB" "VBD" "VBG" "VBN" "VBP" "VBZ" )) )
      (cons
       (quote allupcase)
       (make-array
        2
        :element-type 'string
        :initial-contents  (list "F" "T" )) )
      (cons
       (quote caps)
```

```
(make-array
 3
 :element-type 'string
 :initial-contents (list "lcaps"
                         "sentinitcaps"
                                      "sentmiddlecaps" )) )
(cons
 (quote hyphen)
 (make-array
  2
  :element-type 'string
  :initial-contents  (list "F" "T" )) )
(cons
 (quote inflection)
 (make-array
  7
  :element-type 'string
  :initial-contents  (list "ed" "er" "est" "ing" "ly"
                           "no-inflection" "s" )) )
(cons
 (quote number)
 (make-array
  2
  :element-type 'string
  :initial-contents  (list "F" "T" )) )
(cons
 (quote short)
 (make-array
  2
  :element-type 'string
  :initial-contents  (list "F" "T" )) )
))
```

The second file is an S-PLUS "ASCII data dump" file that contains the smoothed table cell counts. A Common Lisp program groks the data dump file and performs the model evaluation.

References

[Agresti, 1990] Agresti, A. (1990). *Categorical Data Analysis*. John Wiley & Sons, New York.

[Allen, 1995] Allen, J. (1995). *Natural Language Understanding (Second Edition)*. Benjamin/Cummings, Redwood City, CA.

[Alshawi and Carter, 1994] Alshawi, H. and Carter, D. (1994). Training and scaling preference functions for disambiguation. *Computational Linguistics*, 20(4):635–648.

[Altmann, 1989] Altmann, G., editor (1989). *Parsing and Interpretation: Special Issue of Language and Cognitive Processes*, Hove, East Sussex, UK. Lawrence Erlbaum.

[Armstrong, 1994] Armstrong, S., editor (1994). *Using Large Corpora: Papers from the special issues of Computational Linguistics*, Boston, MA. Bradford Books.

[Ash, 1965] Ash, R. (1965). *Information Theory*. Interscience Publishers, New York.

[Bahl et al., 1990a] Bahl, L., Jelinek, F., and Mercer, R. L. (1990a). A maximum likelihood approach to continuous speech recognition. In Waibel, A. and Lee, K.-F., editors, *Readings in Speech Recognition*, pages 308–319, San Mateo, CA. Morgan Kaufman.

[Bahl et al., 1990b] Bahl, L. R., Brown, P. F., de Souza, P. V., and Mercer, R. L. (1990b). A tree-based statistical language model for natural language speech recognition. In Waibel, A. and Lee, K.-F., editors, *Readings in Speech Recognition*, pages 507–514, San Mateo, CA. Morgan Kaufman.

[Bahl and Mercer, 1976] Bahl, L. R. and Mercer, R. L. (1976). Part of speech assignment by a statistical decision algorithm. In *International Symposium on Information Theory*, pages 88–89, Ronneby, Sweden. IEEE.

[Baker, 1976] Baker, J. (1976). *Stochastic Modeling for Speech Recognition*. PhD thesis, Computer Science Department, Carnegie Mellon University, Pittsburgh, PA.

[Bar-Hillel, 1964] Bar-Hillel, Y. (1964). *Language and Information*. Addison-Wesley, Reading, MA.

[Basili et al., 1994] Basili, R., Candito, M. H., Pazienza, M. T., and Velardi, P. (1994). Evaluating the information gain of probability-based PP-disambiguation methods. In *Proceedings of the International Conference on New Mathods in Language Procesing*, pages 101–107, UMIST, Manchester, UK.

[Baum, 1972] Baum, L. E. (1972). An inequality and associated maximization technique in statistical estimation for probabilistic functions of a Markov process. *Inequalities*, (3):1–8.

[Beale, 1988] Beale, A. D. (1988). Lexicon and grammar in probabilistic tagging of written English. In *Proceedings of ACL-88*, pages 211–216.

[Becker et al., 1988] Becker, R. A., Chambers, J. M., and Wilks, A. R. (1988). *The New S language: A Programing Environment for Data Analysis and Graphics.* Wadsworth & Brooks/Cole, Pacific Grove, CA.

[Benello et al., 1989] Benello, J., Mackie, A., and Anderson, J. (1989). Syntactic category disambiguation with neural networks. *Computer Speech and Language,* (3):203–217.

[Bever, 1970] Bever, T. G. (1970). The cognitive basis for linguistic structures. In Hayes, J. R., editor, *Cognition and the Development of Language,* New York. John Wiley.

[Birnbaum, 1985] Birnbaum, L. (1985). Lexical ambiguity as a touchstone for theories of language analysis. In *IJCAI-85,* pages 815–820.

[Bishop et al., 1975] Bishop, Y. M., Fienberg, S. E., and Holland, P. W. (1975). *Discrete Multivariate Analysis: Theory and Practice.* MIT Press, Cambridge, MA.

[Black, 1991] Black, A. (1991). Analysis of unknown words through morphological decomposition. In *Proceedings of EACL-91,* pages 101–106.

[Black et al., 1993] Black, E., Jelinek, F., Lafferty, J., Magerman, D. M., Mercer, R., and Roukos, S. (1993). Towards history-based grammars: Using richer models for probabilistic parsing. In *Proceedings of ACL-93,* pages 31–37.

[Black et al., 1992] Black, E., Jelinek, F., Lafferty, J., Mercer, R., and Roukos, S. (1992). Decision tree models applied to the labeling of text with Parts-of-Speech. In *Proccedings of the Fifth DARPA Speech and Natural Language Workshop,* Harriman, NY.

[Boggess et al., 1991] Boggess, L., Agarwall, R., and Davis, R. (1991). Disambiguation of Prepositional Phrases in automatically labelled technical text. In *AAAI-91,* pages 784–789.

[Boggess III and Boggess, 1994] Boggess III, J. E. and Boggess, L. C. (1994). A hybrid probabilistic/connectionist approach to automatic text tagging. In *Florida AI Research Symposium,* pages 147–151.

[Box and Tiao, 1973] Box, G. E. and Tiao, G. C. (1973). *Bayesian Inference in Statistical Analysis.* Addison-Wesley, Reading, MA.

[Breiman et al., 1984] Breiman, L., Friedman, J., Olshen, R., and Stone, C. (1984). *Classification and Regression Trees.* Wadsworth, Belmont, CA.

[Brent, 1993] Brent, M. (1993). From grammar to lexicon: Unsupervised learning of lexical syntax. *Computational Linguistics,* 19(2):243–262.

[Brill, 1992] Brill, E. (1992). A simple rule-based part of speech tagger. In *Proceedings of the Third Applied Natural Language Processing Conference,* pages 152–155.

[Brill, 1993] Brill, E. (1993). *A Corpus-Based Approach to Language Learning.* PhD thesis, Department of Computer and Information Science, University of Pennsylvania, Philadelphia, PA.

[Brill, 1994] Brill, E. (1994). Some advances in transformation-based part of speech tagging. In *AAAI-94,* pages 722–727.

[Brill and Marcus, 1992] Brill, E. and Marcus, M. (1992). Tagging an unfamiliar text with minimal human supervision. In *Proceedings of the 1992 AAAI Fall Symposium on Probabilistic Approaches to Natural Language, Technical Report FS-92-05,* pages 10–16.

[Brill and Resnik, 1994] Brill, E. and Resnik, P. (1994). A rule-based approach to Prepositional Phrase attachment disambiguation. In *Proceedings of COLING-94,* pages 1198–1204.

[Brown et al., 1992] Brown, P., Pietra, S. D., Pietra, V. D., Lai, J., and Mercer, R. (1992). An estimate of an upper bound for the entropy of English. *Computational Linguistics,* 18(1):31–40.

[Brown et al., 1990] Brown, P. F., Della Pietra, V. J., deSouza, P. V., and Mercer, R. L. (1990). Class-based n-gram models of natural language. *Computational Linguistics*, 18(4):467–480.

[Bruce and Wiebe, 1994a] Bruce, R. and Wiebe, J. (1994a). A new approach to word sense disambiguation. In *ARPA Workshop on Human Language Technology*, pages 244–249, Plainsboro, NJ.

[Bruce and Wiebe, 1994b] Bruce, R. and Wiebe, J. (1994b). Word-sense disambiguation using decomposable models. In *Proceedings of ACL-94*, pages 139–146.

[Carbonell and Hayes, 1987] Carbonell, J. and Hayes, P. (1987). Natural language understanding. In Shapiro, S., editor, *Encyclopedia of Artificial Intelligence*, pages 660–677, New York. Wiley.

[Carbonell, 1979] Carbonell, J. G. (1979). Towards a self-extending parser. In *Proceedings of ACL-79*, pages 3–7.

[Carbonell and Brown, 1988] Carbonell, J. G. and Brown, R. D. (1988). Anaphora resolution: A multi-strategy approach. In *COLING-88*, pages 96–101.

[Carbonell and Hayes, 1983] Carbonell, J. G. and Hayes, P. J. (1983). Recovery strategies for parsing extragrammatical language. *Computational Linguistics*, 9(3-4):123–146.

[Carbonell and Hayes, 1984] Carbonell, J. G. and Hayes, P. J. (1984). Robust parsing using multiple construction-specific strategies. In Bolc, L., editor, *Natural Language Parsing Systems*, pages 1–32. Springer-Verlag, New York.

[Chambers and Hastie, 1992] Chambers, J. M. and Hastie, T. J., editors (1992). *Statistical Models in S*, Pacific Grove, CA. Wadsworth & Brooks/Cole.

[Chang et al., 1992] Chang, J.-S., Luo, Y.-F., and Su, K.-Y. (1992). GPSM: A generalized probabilistic semantic model for ambiguity resolution. In *Proceedings of ACL-92*, pages 177–184.

[Charniak, 1993] Charniak, E. (1993). *Statistical Language Learning*. MIT Press, Cambridge, MA.

[Charniak et al., 1994] Charniak, E., Carroll, G., Adcock, J., Cassandra, A., Gotoh, Y., Katz, J., Littman, M., and McCann, J. (1994). Taggers for parsers. Technical Report CS-94-06, Department of Computer Science, Brown University.

[Charniak et al., 1993] Charniak, E., Hendrickson, C., Jacobson, N., and Perkowitz, M. (1993). Equations for part-of-speech tagging. In *AAAI-93*, pages 784–789.

[Chomsky, 1957] Chomsky, N. (1957). *Syntactic Structures*. Mouton & Co., The Hague.

[Church, 1986] Church, K. (1986). Morphological decomposition and stress assignment for speech syllables. In *Proceedings of ACL-86*, pages 156–164.

[Church et al., 1989] Church, K., Gale, W., Hanks, P., and Hindle, D. (1989). Parsing, word associations and typical predicate-argument relations. In *Proceedings of the First International Workshop on Parsing Technologies*, pages 389–398, Pittsburgh, PA. Carnegie Mellon University.

[Church et al., 1991] Church, K., Gale, W., Hanks, P., and Hindle, D. (1991). Using statistics in lexical analysis. In Zernik, U., editor, *Lexical Acquisition: Using online Resources to Build a Lexicon*, pages 111–158. Lawrence Erlbaum.

[Church, 1980] Church, K. W. (1980). On memory limitations in natural language processing. M.Sc. Thesis.

[Church, 1988] Church, K. W. (1988). A stochastic parts program and Noun Phrase parser for unrestricted text. In *Proceedings of the Second Applied Natural Language Processing Conference*, pages 136–143, Austin, TX.

[Church and Gale, 1989] Church, K. W. and Gale, W. A. (1989). Enhanced Good-Turing and Cat-Cal: Two new estimation methods for estimating probabilities of English bigrams. In *Proceedings of the Second DARPA Speech and Natural Language Workshop*, pages 82–91, Cape Cod, MA. Morgan Kaufman.

[Church and Gale, 1991a] Church, K. W. and Gale, W. A. (1991a). A comparison of the enhanced Good-Turing and deleted estimation methods for estimating probabilities of English bigrams. *Computer Speech and Language*, (5):19–54.

[Church and Gale, 1991b] Church, K. W. and Gale, W. A. (1991b). Probability scoring for spelling correction. *Statistics and Computing*, (1):93–103.

[Church and Hanks, 1990] Church, K. W. and Hanks, P. (1990). Word association norms, mutual information, and lexicography. *Computational Linguistics*, 16(1):22–29.

[Cohen, 1995] Cohen, Paul R. (1995). *Empirical Methods for Artificial Intelligence.* MIT Press, Cambridge, MA.

[Cover and Thomas, 1991] Cover, T. M. and Thomas, J. A. (1991). *Elements of Information Theory.* John Wiley and Sons, New York.

[Crain and Steedman, 1985] Crain, S. and Steedman, M. J. (1985). On not being led up the garden path: The use of context by the psychological syntax processor. In Dowty, D. R., Karttunen, L., and Zwicky, A. M., editors, *Natural Language Parsing*, pages 320–358, Cambridge, UK. Cambridge University Press.

[Crystal, 1985] Crystal, D. (1985). *A Dictionary of Linguistics and Phonetics (2nd Edition).* Basil Blackwell, Oxford, UK.

[Cutting et al., 1992] Cutting, D., Kupiec, J., Pedersen, J., and Sibun, P. (1992). A practical part-of-speech tagger. In *Proceedings of the Third Applied Natural Language Processing Conference*, pages 133–140.

[Dagan et al., 1993] Dagan, I., Marcus, S., and Markovitch, S. (1993). Contextual word similarity and estimation from sparse data. In *Proceedings of ACL-93*, pages 164–171.

[Dagan et al., 1994] Dagan, I., Pereira, F., and Lee, L. (1994). Similarity-based estimation of word cooccurrence probabilities. In *Proceedings of ACL-94*, pages 272–278.

[Dahlgren, 1988] Dahlgren, K. (1988). *Naive Semantics for Natural Language Understanding.* Kluwer, Boston.

[de Marcken, 1990] de Marcken, C. G. (1990). Parsing the LOB corpus. In *Proceedings of ACL-90*, pages 243–251.

[De Mori and Kuhn, 1991] De Mori, R. and Kuhn, R. (1991). Some results on stochastic language modelling. In *Fourth DARPA Workshop on Speech and Natural Language*, pages 225–230, Pacific Grove, CA.

[DeGroot, 1975] DeGroot, M. H. (1975). *Probability and Statistics.* Addison-Wesley, Menlo Park, CA.

[DeGroot, 1986] DeGroot, M. H. (1986). Concepts of information based on utility. In Daboni, L., Montesano, A., and Lines, M., editors, *Recent Developments in the Foundations of Utility and Risk Theory*, pages 265–275. D. Reidel.

[Deming and Stephan, 1940] Deming, W. E. and Stephan, F. F. (1940). On a least squares adjustment of a sampled frequency table when the expected marginal totals are known. *Ann. Math. Statis*, (11):427–444.

[DeRose, 1988] DeRose, S. J. (1988). Grammatical category disambiguation by statistical optimization. *Computational Linguistics*, 14(1):31–39.

[Derouault and Merialdo, 1986] Derouault, A. M. and Merialdo, B. (1986). Natural language modeling for phoneme-to-text transcription. *IEEE TRansactions on Pattern Analysis and Machine Intelligence*, 8(6):742–749.

[Duda and Hart, 1973] Duda, R. O. and Hart, P. E. (1973). *Pattern Classification and Scene Analysis*. John Wiley & Sons, New York.

[Dunning, 1993] Dunning, T. (1993). Accurate methods for the statistics of surprise and coincidence. *Computational Linguistics*, 19(1):61–74.

[Edwards, 1993] Edwards, J. A. (1993). Survey of electronic corpora and related resources for language researchers. In Edwards, J. A. and Lampert, M. D., editors, *Talking data: Transcription and coding in discourse research*. Lawrence Erlbaum, Hillsdale, NJ.

[Eizirik et al., 1993] Eizirik, L. M. R., Barbosa, V. C., and Mendes, S. B. T. (1993). A Bayesian-network approach to lexical disambiguation. *Cognitive Science*, (17):257–283.

[Elbeze and Derouault, 1990] Elbeze, M. and Derouault, A.-M. (1990). A morphological model for large vocabulary speech recognition. In *ICASSP-90*, pages 577–580.

[Elworthy, 1994a] Elworthy, D. (1994a). Automatic error detection in part of speech tagging. In *Proceedings of the International Conference on New Mathods in Language Procesing*, pages 130–135, UMIST, Manchester, UK.

[Elworthy, 1994b] Elworthy, D. (1994b). Does Baum-Welch re-estimation help taggers. In *Proceedings of the Fourth Applied Natural Language Processing Conference*, pages 53–58.

[Erbach, 1990] Erbach, G. (1990). Syntactic processing of unknown words. In Jorrand, P. and Sgurev, V., editors, *Artificial Intelligence IV - methodology, systems, applic ations*, pages 371–382, Amsterdam. North-Holland.

[Fass, 1988] Fass, D. (1988). An account of coherence, semantic relations, metonymy, and lexical ambiguity resolution. In Small, S., Cottrell, G., and Tanenhaus, M., editors, *Lexical Ambiguity Resolution*, pages 151–178, San Mateo, CA. Morgan Kaufmann.

[Ferreti et al., 1990] Ferreti, M., Maltese, G., and Scarci, S. (1990). Measuring information provided by language model and acoustic model in probabilistic speech recognition. *Speech Comunication*, (9):531–539.

[Fienberg, 1980] Fienberg, S. E. (1980). *The Analysis of Cross-Classified Categorical Data*. The MIT Press, Cambridge, MA, second edition edition.

[Finegan and Besnier, 1989] Finegan, E. and Besnier, N. (1989). *Language: Its Structure and Use*. Harcourt Brace Jovanovich, San Diego.

[Firth, 1968] Firth, J. (1968). A synopsis of linguistic theory 1930-1955. In Palmer, F., editor, *Selected Papers of J.R. Firth*, Harlow, UK. Longman.

[Ford et al., 1982] Ford, M., Bresnan, J., and Kaplan, R. (1982). A competence-based theory of syntactic closure. In Bresnan, J. W., editor, *The Mental Representation of Grammatical Relations*, Cambridge, MA. MIT Press.

[Foster, 1991] Foster, G. F. (1991). Statistical lexical disambiguation. Master of science thesis, School of Computer Science, McGill University, Montreal.

[Francis and Kučera, 1982] Francis, W. N. and Kučera, H. (1982). *Frequency Analysis of English Usage*. Houghton Mifflin Company, Boston, MA.

[Franz, 1992] Franz, A. (1992). Ambiguity resolution in natural language parsing. Tecnical Report CMU-CMT-92-135, Center for Machine Translation, Carnegie Mellon University.

[Franz, 1994a] Franz, A. (1994a). Ambiguity resolution via statistical classification: Classifying unknown words by part of speech. Tecnical Report CMU-CMT-94-144, Center for Machine Translation, Carnegie Mellon University.

[Franz, 1994b] Franz, A. (1994b). A statistical method for handling unknown words. In *AAAI-94*, page 1447.

[Franz, 1995a] Franz, A. (1995a). Classifying new words for robust parsing. In *Fifth International Workshop on AI and Statistics*, pages 226–232.

[Franz, 1995b] Franz, A. (1995b). A statistical approach to learning Prepositional Phrase attachment disambiguation. In *IJCAI-95 Workshop on New Approaches to Learning for Natural Language Processing*.

[Frazier and Fodor, 1978] Frazier, L. and Fodor, J. D. (1978). The Sausage machine: A two-stage parsing model. *Cognition*, (6):291–325.

[Frazier, 1979] Frazier, L. (1979). *On Comprehending Sentences: Syntactic Parsing Strategies*. PhD thesis, University of Massachusetts, Amherst, MA.

[Frazier, 1987] Frazier, L. (1987). Sentence processing: A tutorial review. In Coltheart, M., editor, *Attention and Performance XII*, pages 559–586, Hillsdale, NJ. Lawrence Erlbaum.

[Gale and Church, 1994] Gale, W. and Church, K. (1994). What is wrong with adding one? In Oostdijk, N. and de Haan, P., editors, *Corpus-based Research into Language*, pages 189–198, Amsterdam. Rodopi.

[Gale and Church, 1990] Gale, W. A. and Church, K. W. (1990). Poor estimates of context are worse than none. In *Proceedings of the Third DARPA Speech and Natural Language Workshop*, Hidden Valley, PA.

[Gale et al., 1992] Gale, W. A., Church, K. W., and Yarowsky, D. (1992). One sense per discourse. In *Proccedings of the Fifth DARPA Speech and Natural Language Workshop*, Harriman, NY.

[Garnham, 1985] Garnham, A. (1985). Parsing — the computation of syntactic structure. In Garnham, A., editor, *Psycholinguistics: Central Topics*, pages 69–94, New York. Methuen.

[Garside et al., 1987] Garside, R., Leech, G., and Sampson, G. (1987). *The Computational Analysis of English*. Longman, London.

[Gazdar et al., 1987] Gazdar, G., Franz, A., Osborne, K., and Evans, R. (1987). *Natural Language Procesing in the 80s: A Bibliography*, volume 12 of *CSLI Lecture Notes*. Center for the Study of Language and Information, Stanford, CA.

[Gazdar and Mellish, 1989] Gazdar, G. and Mellish, C. (1989). *Natural Language Processing in LISP*. Addison-Wesley, Wokingham, UK.

[Gibson, 1991] Gibson, E. (1991). *A Computational Theory of Human Linguistic Processing: Memory Limitations and Processing Breakdown*. PhD thesis, Computational Linguistics Program, Carnegie Mellon University, Pittsburgh, PA. Published as Technical Report CMU-CMT-91-125.

[Gibson and Pearlmutter, 1994] Gibson, T. and Pearlmutter, N. (1994). A corpus-based analysis of psycholinguistic constraints on PP attachment. In Jr., C. C., Frazier, L., and Rayner, K., editors, *Perspectives on Sentence Processing*. Lawrence Erlbaum Associates.

[Gibson et al., 1993] Gibson, T., Pearlmutter, N., Canseco-Gonzalez, E., and Hickok, G. (1993). Cross-linguistic attachment preferences: Evidence from English and Spanish. Submitted manuscript.

[Good, 1953] Good, I. J. (1953). The population frequencies of species and the estimation of population parameters. *Biometrika*, (40):237–264.

[Good, 1965] Good, I. J. (1965). *The Estimation of Probabilities*. MIT Press, Cambridge, MA.

[Goodman and Nirenburg, 1991] Goodman, K. and Nirenburg, S. (1991). *The KBMT Project: A Case Study in Knowledge-Based Machine Translation*. Morgan Kaufmann, San Mateo, CA.

[Granger, 1977] Granger, R. H. (1977). FOUL-UP: A program that figures out meanings of words from context. In *IJCAI-77*, pages 172–178.

[Green and Rubin, 1971] Green, B. B. and Rubin, G. M. (1971). Automated grammatical tagging of English. Department of Linguistics, Brown University, Providencce, Rhode Island.

[Grishman and Sterling, 1993] Grishman, R. and Sterling, J. (1993). Smoothing of automatically generated selectional constraints. In *ARPA Workshop on Human Language Technology*, Plainsboro, NJ.

[Gupta et al., 1992] Gupta, V., Lennig, M., and Mermelstein, P. (1992). A language model for very large-vocabulary speech recognition. *Computer Speech and Language*, (6):331–344.

[Guthrie et al., 1991] Guthrie, J. A., Guthrie, L., Wilks, Y., and Aidinejad, H. (1991). Subject-dependent co-occurrence and word sense disambiguation. In *Proceedings of ACL-91*, pages 146–152.

[Heeman and Allen, 1994] Heeman, P. A. and Allen, J. (1994). Tagging speech repairs. In *ARPA Workshop on Human Language Technology*, pages 187–192, Plainsboro, NJ.

[Hindle, 1983] Hindle, D. (1983). User manual for Fidditch, a deterministic parser. Technical Memorandum 7590-142, Naval Research Laboratories.

[Hindle, 1989] Hindle, D. (1989). Acquiring disambiguation rules from text. In *Proceedings of ACL-89*, pages 118–125.

[Hindle and Rooth, 1993] Hindle, D. and Rooth, M. (1993). Structural ambiguity and lexical relations. *Computational Linguistics*, 19(1):103–120.

[Hirst, 1986] Hirst, G. (1986). *Semantic Interpretation and the Resolution of Ambiguity*. Cambridge University Press, Cambridge.

[Hoaglin et al., 1983] Hoaglin, D. C., Mosteller, F., and Tukey, J. W. (1983). *Understanding Robust and Exploratory Data Analysis*. John Wiley and Sons, New York.

[Hoaglin et al., 1985] Hoaglin, D. C., Mosteller, F., and Tukey, J. W. (1985). *Exploring Data Tables, Trends, and Shapes*. John Wiley and Sons, New York.

[Hobbs and Bear, 1990] Hobbs, J. R. and Bear, J. (1990). Two principles of parse preference. In *Proceedings of COLING-90*, pages 162–167.

[Hobson and Cheng, 1973] Hobson, A. and Cheng, B.-K. (1973). A comparison of the Shannon and Kullback information measures. *Journal of Statistical Physics*, 7(4):301–310.

[Horrocks, 1987] Horrocks, G. (1987). *Generative Grammar*. Longman, Essex, UK.

[Isotani and Matsunaga, 1994] Isotani, R. and Matsunaga, S. (1994). Speech recognition using a stochastic language model integrating local and global constraints. In *ARPA Workshop on Human Language Technology*, pages 21–24, Plainsboro, NJ.

[Jacobs et al., 1991] Jacobs, P. S., Krupka, G. R., and Rau, L. F. (1991). Lexico-semantic pattern matching as a companion to parsing in text understanding. In *Proceedings of the Fourth DARPA Speech and Natural Language Workshop*, pages 337–342, Pacific Grove, CA.

[Jelinek, 1985] Jelinek, F. (1985). Markov source modeling of text generation. In Skwirzinski, J. K., editor, *The Impact of Processing Techniques on Communication*. Nijhoff, Dordrecht.

[Jelinek, 1990] Jelinek, F. (1990). Self-organized language modeling for speech recognition. In Waibel, A. and Lee, K.-F., editors, *Readings in Speech Recognition*, pages 450–506, San Mateo, CA. Morgan Kaufman.

[Jelinek, 1991] Jelinek, F. (1991). Up from Trigrams! The struggle for improved language models. In *Eurospeech-91*, pages 1037–1040.

[Jelinek et al., 1990] Jelinek, F., Lafferty, J. D., and Mercer, R. L. (1990). Basic methods of probabilistic context free grammars. Research Report RC 16374, IBM Research Division, T.J. Watson Research Center, Yorktown Heights, NY.

[Jelinek and Mercer, 1985] Jelinek, F. and Mercer, R. (1985). Probability distribution estimation from sparse data. *IBM Technical Disclosure Bulletin*, (28):2591–2594.

[Jelinek and Mercer, 1980] Jelinek, F. and Mercer, R. L. (1980). Interpolated estimation of Markov source parameters from sparse data. In Gelsema, E. and Kanal, L., editors, *Pattern Recognition in Practice*, pages 381–397, Amsterdam. North-Holland.

[Jelinek et al., 1977] Jelinek, F., Mercer, R. L., Bahl, L. R., and J, K. B. (1977). Perplexity — a measure of difficulty of speech recognition tasks. In *94th Meeting of the Acoustical Society of America*, Miami Beach, FL.

[Jensen and Binot, 1988] Jensen, K. and Binot, J.-L. (1988). Dictionary text entries as a source of knowledge for syntactic and other disambiguations. In *Proceedings of the Second Conference on Applied Natural Language Processing*, pages 152–159. Association for Computational Linguistics.

[Jensen et al., 1983] Jensen, K., Heidorn, G., Miller, L., and Ravin, Y. (1983). Parse fitting and prose fixing: Getting a hold on ill-formedness. *Computational Linguistics*, 9(3-4):147–160.

[Jensen et al., 1993] Jensen, K., Heidorn, G. E., and Richardson, S. D. (1993). *Natural Language Processing: The PLNLP Approach*. Kluwer, Boston, MA.

[Kakagahara and Aizawa, 1988] Kakagahara, K. and Aizawa, T. (1988). Completion of Japanese sentences by inferring function words from content words. In *Proceedings of COLING-88*, pages 291–296.

[Katz and Fodor, 1963] Katz, J. and Fodor, J. (1963). The structure of a semantic theory. *Language*, (39):170–210.

[Katz, 1987] Katz, S. (1987). Estimation of probabilities from sparse data for the language model component of a speech recognizer. *IEEE Transactions on Acoustics, Speech, and Signal Processing*, ASSP-35(3).

[Kimball, 1973] Kimball, J. (1973). Seven principles of surface structure parsing in natural language. *Cognition*, (2):15–47.

[Kitano, 1994] Kitano, H. (1994). *Speech-speech Translation: A Massively Parallel Memory-based Approach*. Kluwer Academic Press, Boston, MA.

[Kitano et al., 1989] Kitano, H., Tomabechi, H., and Levin, L. (1989). Ambiguity resolution in the DMTRANS PLUS. In *Proceedings of the Fourth Conference of the European Chapter of the Association for Computational Linguistics*, Manchester.

[Klein and Simmons, 1963] Klein, S. and Simmons, R. (1963). A computational approach to grammatical coding of English words. *JACM*, (10).

[Knight, 1987] Knight, K. (1987). TREEPRINT: A program that draws parse trees. Tecnical Memo CMU-CMT-87-MEMO, Center for Machine Translation, Carnegie Mellon University.

[Koskenniemi, 1990] Koskenniemi, K. (1990). Finite-state parsing and disambiguation. In *Proceedings of COLING-90*, pages 229–232.

[Krovetz and Croft, 1992] Krovetz, R. and Croft, W. B. (1992). Lexcical ambiguity and information retrieval. *ACM Transactions in Information Systems*, 10(2):115–141.

[Kuhn and Mori, 1990] Kuhn, R. and Mori, R. D. (1990). A cache-based Natural Language model for speech recognition. *IEEE Transactions on Pattern Analysis and Machine Intelligence*, 12(6):570–583.

[Kullback, 1951] Kullback, S. (1951). *Information Theory and Statistics*. Wiley, New York.

[Kupiec, 1992] Kupiec, J. (1992). Robust part-of-speech tagging using a hidden Markov model. *Computer Speech and Language*, (6):225–242.

[Lafrance, 1990] Lafrance, P. (1990). *Fundamental Concepts in Communication*. Prentice-Hall, Englewood Cliffs, NJ.

[Lee, 1986] Lee, K.-F. (1986). A pattern classification approach to evaluation function learning. Tecnical Report CMU-CS-86-173, CMU.

[Levinson et al., 1983] Levinson, S., Rabiner, L., and Sondhi, M. (1983). An introduction to the application of probabilistic functions of a Markov process to automatic speech recognition. *Bell Systems Technical Journal*, 62(1035).

[Lin et al., 1995] Lin, Y.-C., Chiang, T.-H., and Su, K.-Y. (1995). The effects of learning, parameter tying and model refinement for improving probabilistic tagging. *Computer Speech and Language*, (9):37–61.

[Macklovitch, 1992] Macklovitch, E. (1992). Where the tagger falters. In *Proceedings of the Fourth International Conference on Theoretical Issues in Machine Translation*, pages 113–126, Montreal, Canada.

[Magerman, 1994] Magerman, D. (1994). *Natural Language Parsing as Statistical Pattern Recognition*. PhD thesis, Department of Computer Science, Stanford University, Stanford, CA.

[Magerman and Marcus, 1990] Magerman, D. and Marcus, M. (1990). Parsing a natural language using mutual information statistics. In *AAAI-90*.

[Magerman and Marcus, 1991] Magerman, D. M. and Marcus, M. P. (1991). PEARL: A probabilistic chart parser. In *Proceedings of the Second International Workshop on Parsing Technologies*, pages 193–199.

[Manning, 1993] Manning, C. (1993). Automatic acquisition of a large subcategorization dictionary from corpora. In *Proceedings of ACL-93*, pages 235–242.

[Mansuripur, 1987] Mansuripur, M. (1987). *Introduction to Information Theory*. Prentice-Hall International, London.

[Marcus, 1980] Marcus, M. (1980). *A Theory of Syntactic Recognition for Natural Language*. MIT Press, Cambridge, MA.

[Marcus et al., 1993] Marcus, M. P., Santorini, B., and Marcinkiewicz, M. A. (1993). Building a large annotated corpus of English: The Penn Treebank. *Computational Linguistics*, 19(2):313–330.

[Markov, 1913] Markov, A. (1913). An example of statistical investigation in the text of "Eugene Onyegin" illustrating coupling of tests in chains. *Proceedings of the Academy of Science of St. Petersburg, VI Ser.*, 7(153).

[Martin et al., 1981] Martin, W. A., Church, K. W., and Patil, R. S. (1981). Preliminary analysis of a breadth-first parsing algorithm: Theoretical and experimental results. Report TR-261, MIT LCS.

[Matsukawa et al., 1993] Matsukawa, T., Miller, S., and Weischedel, R. (1993). Example-based correction of word segmentation and part of speech labelling. In *ARPA Workshop on Human Language Technology*, pages 227–232, Plainsboro, NJ.

[Mauldin, 1991] Mauldin, M. (1991). *Conceptual Information Retrieval: A Case Study in Adaptive Partial Parsing*. Kluwer Academic Press, Boston, MA.

[Merialdo, 1994] Merialdo, B. (1994). Tagging English text with a probabilistic model. *Computational Linguistics*, 20(2):155–171.

[Meteer et al., 1991] Meteer, M., Schwartz, R., and Weischedel, R. (1991). POST: Using probabilities in language processing. In *IJCAI-91*, pages 960–965.

[Morgan, 1968] Morgan, B. W. (1968). *An Introduction to Bayesian Statistical Processes*. Prentice-Hall, Englewood Cliffs, NJ.

[Mosteller and Wallace, 1984] Mosteller, F. and Wallace, D. L. (1984). *Applied Bayesian and Classical Inference: The Case of* THE FEDERALIST *Papers (2nd Edition of* INFERENCE AND DISPUTED AUTHORSHIP: THE FEDERALIST*)*. Springer Verlag, New York.

[Nadas, 1984] Nadas, A. (1984). Estimation of probabilities in the language model of the IBM speech recognition system. *IEEE Transactions on Acoustics, Speech, and Signal Processing*, ASSP-32:859–861.

[Nadas, 1985] Nadas, A. (1985). On Turing's formula for word probabilities. *IEEE Transactions on Acoustics, Speech, and Signal Processing*, ASSP-33:1414–1416.

[Nagao, 1990] Nagao, K. (1990). Dependency analyzer: A knowledge-based approach to structiral disambiguation. In *Proceedings of COLING-90*, pages 282–287.

[Nakamura et al., 1990] Nakamura, M., Maruyama, K., Kawabata, T., and Shikano, K. (1990). Neural network approach to word category prediction for English texts. In *Proceedings of COLING-90*, pages 213–218.

[Nakamura and Shikano, 1989] Nakamura, M. and Shikano, K. (1989). A study of English word category prediction based on neural networks. In *ICASSP-89*, pages 731–734.

[Nakhimovsky, 1990] Nakhimovsky, A. (1990). A lexicon-based algorithm for ambiguity resolution in parsing. In Steele, J., editor, *Meaning-text theory: Linguistics, Lexicography, and Implications*, pages 327–349, Ottawa. University of Ottawa Press.

[Newmeyer, 1988] Newmeyer, F. J., editor (1988). *Linguistics: The Cambridge Survey*, Cambridge, UK. Cambridge University Press.

[Ney and Nessen, 1991] Ney, H. and Nessen, U. (1991). On smoothing techniques for bigram-based natural language modelling. In *ICASSP-91*, pages 825–828.

[Niv, 1993] Niv, M. (1993). *A Computational Model of Syntactic Processing: Ambiguity Resolution from Interpretation*. PhD thesis, Department of Computer and Information Science, University of Pennsylvania, Philadelpia, PA.

[O'Grady et al., 1989] O'Grady, W., Dobrovolsky, M., and Aronoff, M. (1989). *Contemporary Linguistics: An Introduction*. St. Martin's Press, New York.

[O'Shaughnessy, 1989] O'Shaughnessy, D. (1989). Using syntactic information to improve large-vocabulary word recognition. In *ICASSP-89*, pages 715–718.

[Paul, 1990] Paul, D. (1990). Speech recognition using Hidden Markov Models. *Lincoln Laboratory Journal*, 3(1):41–62.

[Pearl, 1988] Pearl, J. (1988). *Probabilistic Reasoning in Intelligent Systems*. Morgan Kaufmann, San Mateo, CA.

[Pereira et al., 1993] Pereira, F., Tishby, N., and Lee, L. (1993). Distributional clustering of English words. In *Proceedings of ACL-93*, pages 183–190.

[Pereira, 1985] Pereira, F. C. (1985). A new characterization of attachment preferences. In Dowty, D. R., Karttunen, L., and Zwicky, A. M., editors, *Natural Language Parsing*, pages 307–319, Cambridge, UK. Cambridge University Press.

[Pierce, 1980] Pierce, J. R. (1980). *An Introduction to Information Theory (Seond Edition)*. Dover, New York.

[Pollard, 1988] Pollard, C. (1988). The nature and structure of a computational linguistic theory. In *Proceedings of the R.O.C Computational Linguistics Workshop I*, pages 291–318.

[Pollard and Sag, 1987] Pollard, C. and Sag, I. (1987). *Information-Based Syntax and Semantics: Volume 1, Fundamentals*, volume 13 of *CSLI Lecture Series*. CSLI, Stanford, CA.

[Pollard and Sag, 1994] Pollard, C. and Sag, I. (1994). *Head-driven phrase structure grammar*. University of Chicago Press, Chicago.

[Quirk and Greenbaum, 1973] Quirk, R. and Greenbaum, S. (1973). *A University Grammar of English*. Longman, London.

[Quirk et al., 1985] Quirk, R., Greenbaum, S., Leech, G., and Svartik, J. (1985). *A Comprehensive Grammar of the English Language*. Longman, London.

[Rabiner, 1990] Rabiner, L. R. (1990). A tutorial on Hidden Markov Models and selected applications in speech recognition. In Waibel, A. and Lee, K.-F., editors, *Readings in Speech Recognition*, pages 267–296, San Mateo, CA. Morgan Kaufman.

[Ramshaw and Marcus, 1994] Ramshaw, L. A. and Marcus, M. P. (1994). Exploring the statistical derivation of transformational rule sequences for part-of-speech tagging. In *Proceedings of ACL-94*, pages 86–95.

[Ratnaparkhi et al., 1994] Ratnaparkhi, A., Rynar, J., and Roukos, S. (1994). A maximum entropy model for Prepositional Phrase attachment. In *ARPA Workshop on Human Language Technology*, Plainsboro, NJ.

[Resnik, 1992] Resnik, P. (1992). WORDNET and distributional analysis: A class-based approach to lexical discovery. In *Proceedings of the 1992 AAAI Workshop on Statistically-Based Natural Language Programming Techniques, Technical Report W-92-01*, pages 48–56.

[Resnik, 1993a] Resnik, P. (1993a). *Selection and Information: A Class-based Approach to Lexical Relationships*. PhD thesis, Department of Computer and Information Science, University of Pennsylvania, Philadelphia, PA.

[Resnik, 1993b] Resnik, P. (1993b). Semantic classes and syntactic ambiguity. In *ARPA Workshop on Human Language Technology*, Plainsboro, NJ.

[Resnik and Hearst, 1993] Resnik, P. and Hearst, M. (1993). Structural ambiguity and conceptual relations. In *Proceedings of the Workshop on Very Large Corpora*, pages 58–64.

[Richardson et al., 1993] Richardson, S., Vanderwende, L., and Dolan, W. (1993). Combining dictionary-based methods for natural language analysis. In *Fifth International Conference on Theoretical and Methodological Isues in Machine Tranlation*, pages 69–79, Kyoto, Japan.

[Riesbeck, 1987] Riesbeck, C. (1987). Expectation-driven parsing. In Shapiro, S., editor, *Encyclopedia of Artificial Intelligence*, pages 696–701, New York. Wiley.

[Saffiotti, 1987] Saffiotti, A. (1987). An AI view of the treatment of uncertainty. *The Knowledge Engineering Review*, 2(2):57–97.

[Santorini, 1991a] Santorini, B. (1991a). Bracketing guidelines for the Penn Treebank project. University of Pennsylvania.

[Santorini, 1991b] Santorini, B. (1991b). Part-of-speech tagging guidelines for the Penn Treebank project. University of Pennsylvania.

[Schank, 1975] Schank, R. C. (1975). *Conceptual Information Processing*. North Holland, Amsterdam.

[Schank and Abelson, 1977] Schank, R. C. and Abelson, R. P. (1977). *Scripts, Plans, Goals, and Understanding*. Lawrence Erlbaum, Hillside, NJ.

[Schmid, 1994a] Schmid, H. (1994a). Part-of-speeech tagging with neural networks. In *Proceedings of COLING-94*, pages 172–176.

[Schmid, 1994b] Schmid, H. (1994b). Probabilistic part-of-specch tagging using decision trees. In *Proceedings of the International Conference on New Mathods in Language Procesing*, pages 44–49, UMIST, Manchester, UK.

[Schuetze, 1993a] Schuetze, H. (1993a). Distributed syntactic representations with an application to part-of-speech tagging. In *Proceedings of the IEEE International Conference on Neural Networks*.

[Schuetze, 1993b] Schuetze, H. (1993b). Part-of-speech induction from scratch. In *Proceedings of ACL-93*, pages 251–258.

[Schuetze and Singer, 1994] Schuetze, H. and Singer, Y. (1994). Part-of-speech tagging using a variable memory Markov model. In *Proceedings of ACL-94*, pages 181–187.

[Seidenfeld, 1986] Seidenfeld, T. (1986). Entropy and uncertainty. *Philosophy of Science*, 53(4):467–491.

[Sells, 1985] Sells, P. (1985). *Lectures on Contemporary Linguistic Theories*, volume 3 of *CSLI Lecture Notes*. Center for the Study of Language and Information, Stanford, CA.

[Seneff, 1992] Seneff, S. (1992). TINA: A natural language system for spoken language applications. *Computational Linguistics*, 18(1):61–86.

[Shannon, 1948] Shannon, C. (1948). A mathematical theory of communication. *Bell System Technical Journal*, (27):623–656.

[Shannon, 1951] Shannon, C. E. (1951). Prediction and entropy of printed English. In *Proceedings of the IEEE International Conference on Neural Networks*.

[Shieber, 1983] Shieber, S. (1983). Sentence disambiguation by a shift-reduce parsing technique. In *Proceedings of ACL-83*, pages 113–118.

[Smadja, 1991] Smadja, F. (1991). Macrocoding the lexicon with co-occurence knowledge. In Zernik, U., editor, *Lexical Acquisition: Using on-line Resources to Build a Lexicon*, pages 165–189. Lawrence Erlbaum.

[Smadja, 1993] Smadja, F. (1993). Retrieving collocations from text: XTRACT. *Computational Linguistics*, 19(1):143–178.

[Small, 1980] Small, S. (1980). Word expert parsing. Technical Report 945, Computer Science Department, University of Maryland.

[Small et al., 1988] Small, S., Cottrell, G., and Tanenhaus, M. (1988). *Lexical Ambiguity Resolution: Perspectives from Psycholinguistics, Neuropsychology, and Artificial Intelligence*. Morgan Kaufmann, San Mateo, CA.

[Statistical Sciences, Inc., 1991a] Statistical Sciences, Inc. (1991a). S-plus reference manual, version 3.0. Technical report, Seattle, WA.

[Statistical Sciences, Inc., 1991b] Statistical Sciences, Inc. (1991b). S-plus user's manual. Version 3.0, Seattle, WA.

[Sumita et al., 1993] Sumita, E., Furuse, O., and Iida, H. (1993). An example-based disambiguation of Prepositional Phrase attachment. In *Fifth International Conference on Theoretical and Methodological Issues in Machine Tranlation*, pages 80–91, Kyoto, Japan.

[Tapanainen and Voutilainen, 1994] Tapanainen, P. and Voutilainen, A. (1994). Tagging accurately - don't guess if you know. In *Proceedings of the Fourth Applied Natural Language Processing Conference*, pages 47–52.

[Taraban, 1988] Taraban, R. M. (1988). *Content-nased expactations: One source of guidance for syntactic attachment and thematic role assignment in sentence processing*. PhD thesis, Department of English, Carnegie Mellon University, Pittsburgh, PA. Published as Technical Report CMU-CMT-91-125.

[Taraban et al., 1990] Taraban, R. M. and McClelland, J. R. (1990). Parsing and comprehension: A multiple constraint view. In Balota, D. A., Flores d'Arcais, G. B., and Rayner, K., editors, *Comprehension Processes in Reading*, Lawrence Erlbaum Associates.

[Touretzky, 1988] Touretzky, D. S. (1988). Connectionism and PP attachment. In Touretzky, D., Hinton, G., and Sejnowski, T., editors, *Proceedings of the 1988 Connectionist Summer School*, pages 325–332. Morgan Kaufmann.

[Tribus and Rossi, 1993] Tribus, M. and Rossi, R. (1993). On the Kullback information measure as a basis for information theory: Comments on a proposal by Hobson and Chang. *Journal of Statistical Physics*, 9(4):331–338.

[Trueswell et al., 1994] Trueswell and Tanenhaus (1994). A corpus-based analysis of psycholinguistic constraints on Prepositional Phrase attachment. In Clifton Jr., C., Frazier, L. and Rayner, K., editors, *Perspectives on Sentence Processing*, Lawrence Erlbaum Associates.

[Tukey, 1977] Tukey, J. (1977). *Exploratory Data Analysis*. Addison-Wesley, Reading, MA.

[Ueberla, 1994] Ueberla, J. (1994). *Analyzing and Improving Statistical Language Models for Speech Recognition*. PhD thesis, School of Computer Science, Simon Fraser University.

[Ushioda et al., 1993] Ushioda, A., Evans, D. A., Gibson, T., and Waibel, A. (1993). The automatic acquisition of frequencies of verb subcategorization frames from tagged corpora. In Boguraev, B. and Pustejovsky, J., editors, *Acquisition of Lexical Knowledge from Text, Proceedings of the SIGLEX ACL Workshop,* pages 95–106.

[Velleman, 1993] Velleman, P. F. (1993). *Learning Data Analysis with Data Desk.* W.H. Freeman and Company, New York.

[Viterbi, 1967] Viterbi, A. J. (1967). Error bounds for convolutional codes and an asymptotically optimal decoding algorithm. *IEEE Transactions on Information Theory,* (IT-13):260–269.

[Waibel and Lee, 1990] Waibel, A. and Lee, K.-F., editors (1990). *Readings in Speech Recognition,* San Mateo, CA. Morgan Kaufman.

[Weischedel et al., 1993] Weischedel, R., Meteer, M., Schwartz, R., Ramshaw, L., and Palmucci, J. (1993). Coping with ambiguity and unknown words through probabilistic models. *Computational Linguistics,* 19(2):359–382.

[Whittemore et al., 1990] Whittemore, G., Ferrara, K., and Brunner, H. (1990). Empirical study of predictive powers of simple attachment schemes for post-modifier Prepositional Phrases. In *Proceedings of ACL-90,* pages 23–30.

[Wilks et al., 1990] Wilks, Y. A., Fass, D., Guo, C.-M., McDonald, J. E., Plate, T., and Slator, B. M. (1990). Providing machine-tractable dictionary tools. *Machine Translation,* (5):99–154.

[Winograd, 1983] Winograd, T. (1983). *Language as a Cognitive Process: Syntax.* Addison-Wesley, Reading, MA.

[Zernik, 1991] Zernik, U. (1991). Tagging word sense in a corpus. In Zernik, U., editor, *Lexical Acquisition: Using on-line Resources to Build a Lexicon,* pages 97–112. Lawrence Erlbaum.

[Zernik, 1992] Zernik, U. (1992). Shipping departments vs. shipping pacemakers: Using thematic analysis to improve tagging accuracy. In *AAAI-92,* pages 335–342.

[Zipf, 1949] Zipf, G. (1949). *Human Behavior and the Principle of Least Effort.* Addison-Wesley, Cambridge, MA.

Index

Springer
and the
environment

At Springer we firmly believe that an international science publisher has a special obligation to the environment, and our corporate policies consistently reflect this conviction.

We also expect our business partners – paper mills, printers, packaging manufacturers, etc. – to commit themselves to using materials and production processes that do not harm the environment. The paper in this book is made from low- or no-chlorine pulp and is acid free, in conformance with international standards for paper permanency.

 Springer

Lecture Notes in Artificial Intelligence (LNAI)

Lecture Notes in Computer Science